Pinyon Review

Celebrating the Arts & Sciences

May 2012 • Number 1

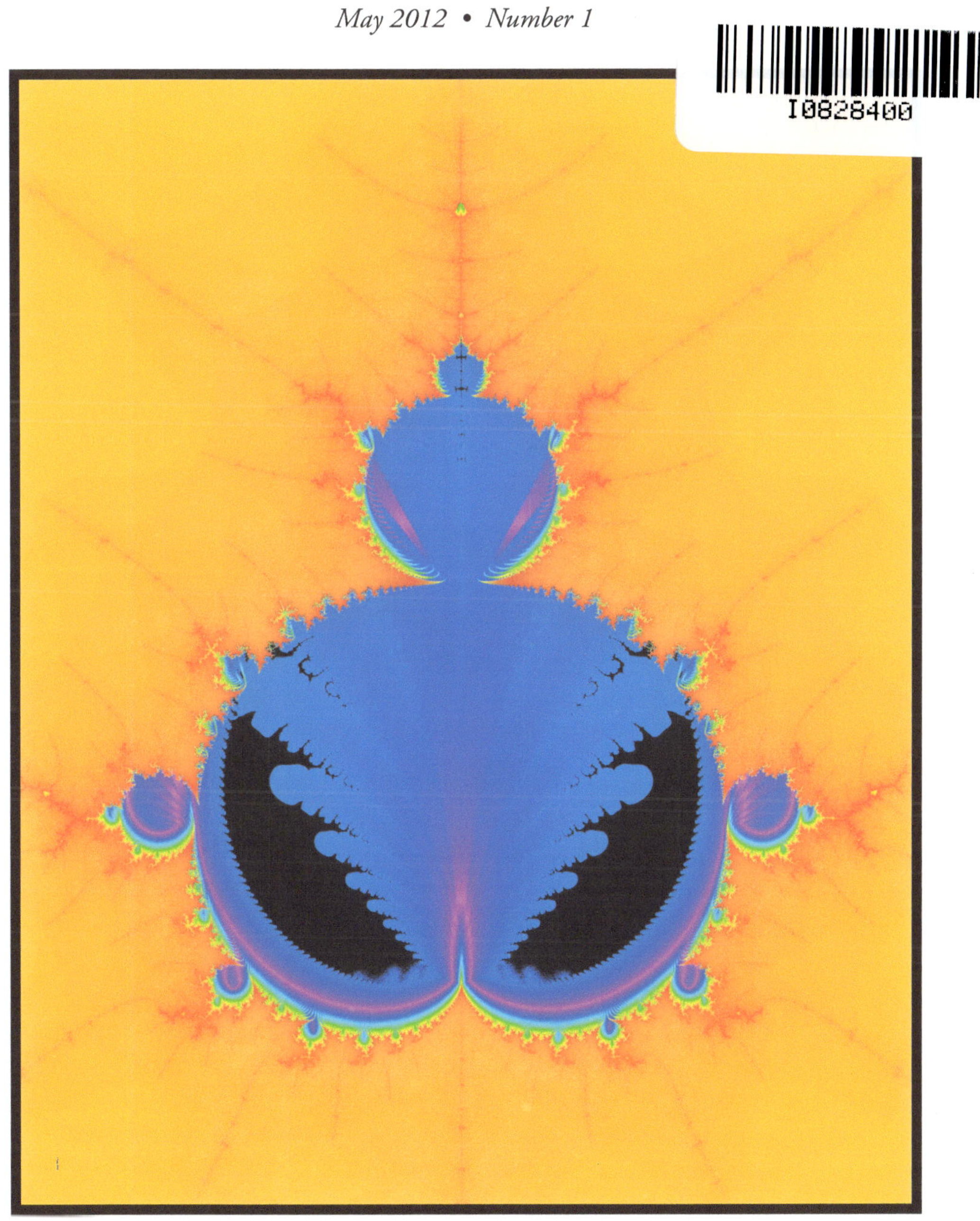

Mandelbrot Set Fractal by Larry Fogg

EDITOR
Gary Lee Entsminger

MANAGING EDITOR
Susan Elizabeth Elliott

Book and Cover Design by Susan E. Elliott

Pinyon Publishing
23847 V66 Trail, Montrose, CO 81403
www.pinyon-publishing.com

ISBN: 978-1-936671-09-0

CONTENTS

GARY L. ENTSMINGER

The Fool on the Hill

For our first issue we're pleased to have several long-time friends contributing. Dabney Stuart has been my literary mentor since the 1970s. Cy Dillon and I were students together at Washington & Lee University. Larry Fogg and I edited (along with David Thompson) one of the earliest microcomputer journals, *Micro Cornucopia,* in the 1980s. Larry's fine essay on fractal geometry is a mellow blend of science, math, computer programming, and art. Larry's computer-generated fractals and Susan Elliott's exquisite watercolor paintings are contrasting, yet fine companions of art.

We're also delighted to have poems by award-winning poets: Ken Fontenot, Diane Moore, Luci Shaw, Dabney Stuart, Don Thompson, and Francine Marie Tolf.

The feature for our first issue is exceptionally fit to "celebrate the arts and sciences." *Coulter Country* was written in 1967 by Dr. Gerald L. Brody, who was a pathologist by profession, as well as an amateur ornithologist, expert fly fisherman, and outdoor enthusiast. He also wrote about his adventures and submitted *Coulter Country* to *Esquire Magazine* in May of 1967, 45 years ago. The editor was enthusiastic about the story but had a backlog of "pieces on angling" yet went on to suggest a book of essays, which Dr. Brody started but didn't complete, and the individual essays remained unpublished. *Coulter Country* does contain choice descriptions of angling. But more, it's a story about an innovative, recently married couple's hiking and personal adventure into a remote wilderness of Wyoming. Anyone who hikes or backpacks today in the US will see how much has changed in a short time.

Coulter Country is accompanied by a soundtrack of sorts, a story by southern California writer, Jack Starr, that echoes the music and mood of 1967, when Brian Wilson's and Van Dyke Parks' classic, *Heroes and Villains,* was released on the Beach Boys' *Smiley Smile* album. Starr's story, like Brian Wilson's music, is structurally simple yet overlaid with chromatic arrangements.

DABNEY STUART

Everywhere lost

Everywhere lost the old poet writes.
His brush hovers over the last stroke.

From his table he looks down a ridge of pines
to the river where sun spots dance in the riffles.

He is taken with people who resign from positions
they have spent much of their lives studying for
to come to the mountains and whittle ducks.

He angles his brush against the ink stand,
tends his small stove, stands by the window.

A hawk settles on a pine bough
which sways a little with the extra weight.
His tail feathers focus light as he flies off.

Everywhere, he thinks, and walks out
to the gate he keeps open, rests his hand on it.
Sun catches the gray hairs on his forearm.

Having the dead to breakfast

Having the dead to breakfast, eggs and bacon,
wheat toast with homemade lemon marmalade.

They are polite and friendly at the same time,
asking about the grandchildren, the garden,
the tangible ingredients of our lives.

They seem almost to breathe the hyacinth blue air.

When the sun rises they are no longer there,
sipping coffee, being confidential,
running a finger down the side of a glass.

Office

The day I said goodbye to my modest
university office, I stood still
in the middle of it, door closed.

The time of day didn't register—the usual dust
seemed no more than what I had breathed daily,
a professor's legacy—but it must

have been late afternoon in the half light,
whatever that is, settled on the panes
of the influential window. I looked at it.

I looked at the ceiling, the plastic honeycomb
cover on its fluorescent centerpiece. For almost
forty years it had kept my bald head warm.

Now it became the axis on which I tracked,
not dancing exactly—I don't know how—
but turning in place, arms out like a Greek

in a taverna, my rhythmic motion
blent with the lost hours of the place, lifted
from me in the lifelong art of becoming gone.

I enlarged my orbit until I touched the walls.
I sat on the desk in passing. I swiveled
the chair. I ran my fingers through the knell

the empty shelves cast into the air.
It was a blessing I bestowed on myself,
made pure by my knowing I didn't care

beyond this strange, contained farewell
which was also a greeting, a blending
of selves and time, not a eulogy or a toll

but a toast. I stopped, back in the center,
set my hands in a steeple under my heart,
bowed. Then I opened the door

quietly, the one I had passed through those years
ago, and through those years, only the one door,
and left, taking back all my entrances.

GERALD L. BRODY

Coulter Country

"August 15, 1806

Colter one of our men expressed a desire to join Some trappers [the two Illinois Men we met, & who now came down to us] *who offered to become shearers with [him] and furnish traps &c. the offer [was] a very advantagious one, to him, his services could be dispenced with from this down and as we were disposed to be of service to any one of our party who had performed their duty as well as Colder had done, we agreed to allow him the privilage provided no one of the party would ask or expect a Similar permission to which they all agreed that they wished Colter every suckcess and that as we did not wish any of them to Seperate untill we Should arive at St. Louis they would not apply or expect it &c. great number of the nativs of the different villages came to view us and exchange robes with our men for their Skins we gave Jo Colter Some Small articles which we did not want and some powder and lead. the party also gave him several articles which will be usefull to him on his expedittion."*

—The Journals of Lewis and Clark[1]

"Thump-thump, thump-thump."

"What the heck is that?" I was awakened from a sound sleep by the measured sounds. I rolled over in the sleeping bag, cocked myself up on my elbows, and peered out through the mosquito netting that covered the door of the tent. About twenty-five yards away a cow elk was running to and fro in the meadow, stopping every now and then to peer at our vinyl shelter, trying to figure out what it was. As it was dark green and brown, only four feet high at the front, and pitched against a lodgepole pine, it made a perfect blind. I poked my wife, Iris, in the ribs, "Hey, kiddo wake up; we've got company." We lay there side by side for a bit watching the elk. She trotted lightly with beautiful action, her head held high with her nose pointed slightly upward. She simply couldn't make out what we were. After a short while

1 DeVoto, B., ed., *The Journals of Lewis and Clark* (Boston: Hougton Mifflin, 1953).

she trotted off, Iris went back to sleep as it was only 5:30 in the morning, and I continued to stare out at the meadow watching the early morning mist swirl gently about. We were in the heart of Coulter's country, and as I lay there I thought of the long chain of events that brought us here.

After seven years of canoe tripping in Canada, I was quite content with the notion that I was an experienced and competent camper. In Ann Arbor, however, I met a man who had systematically studied camping methods since his boyhood. Meeting my mentor, Bud Littler, camping with him, discussing camping methods with him over many a long campfire, soon convinced me of the error of my ways and, after a while, I became equally certain that I was no camper at all. For Bud is an expert—the sort who plunges into the woods during a winter cold snap, his only shelter a four-by-six-foot nylon tarpaulin, to camp alone several days in the snow. His apparently abandoned car at the end of lonely roads in midwinter has provoked more than one phone call by concerned deputy sheriffs who inquire of his wife if he's missing.

Camping can be divided into a number of categories which, in large part, relate to the restrictions on the gear to be carried by the camper. Easiest of all is horse packing. The camper carries nothing; the horse carries all. In fact, the camper doesn't even have to walk. The only limitation is the budget. If he wishes to lug along the kitchen stove, it can be arranged provided he has money enough to hire a sufficient number of pack horses. To be sure, the horses need caring for and one must know how to wrangle and pack them, but usually this is done by the packer who runs the stock.

Even easier than horse packing is car camping in which one pulls up to a campground and gets his gear out of the trunk or off a rack on the roof. But in Bud's and my biased estimation, this hardly qualifies as camping. It's fine for a weekend and for escaping motel bills, but let it not be called "true camping." In state and national parks one now sees electric utility poles into which "campers" plug portable TV sets. The viewers cannot tear themselves away even when on vacation. Surely, this is not camping. We have heard teenagers listening to three different rock and roll music programs simultaneously on three transistor radios while "camping."

Next in line after horse packing comes canoe tripping. As the horse packer must know how to handle a horse, so must the canoe tripper know how to manage a canoe. But after that, the two methods diverge sharply in the demands put on the camper. On portage canoes must be flipped and carried. The lightest aluminum canoes weigh about forty-five pounds, although a standard fifteen- or sixteen-foot model weighs about sixty. Wooden and canvas canoes are much heavier; I once used an eighteen-footer that weighed one hundred and thirty pounds! A sixteen-foot Chestnut canoe will weigh about seventy to eighty pounds depending upon how tight its canvas is and how much water it has picked up. Immediately therefore, the canoe tripper has a burden. Furthermore, whatever he takes with him in the way of food, clothing, equipment, and shelter, he must backpack over the portages. Those are the limitations of this kind of camping. On the other hand, when he is not portaging, the canoe carries his goods, and the only effort required of him is the paddling which becomes automatic and easier than walking once it has been properly learned. It goes without saying that both riding a horse and paddling a canoe are distinct delights in themselves; they are much, much more than merely the means to the ends of "getting there" and are added dividends in these two forms of outdoor activity.

The most demanding form of camping is backpacking. Here there is no surcease—one's burdens are ever with him. He cannot escape them unless he chooses to starve, freeze, or both. It follows then that the backpacker must have the greatest expertise in knowing how to get the most out of the least. He must learn how to cut corners, to discard ruthlessly all but absolute necessities, to measure in ounces rather than pounds to make his pack as light as possible. Now *he* is the horse, *he* is the canoe, and that pack will be ever on his back. What is more, camping equipment suitable for horse packing or canoe tripping may be totally unsuitable for hiking and backpacking because of its weight and bulk. The reverse is not true, however, and equipment suitable for backpacking will work perfectly well on the other kinds of trips. The backpacker must use none but the lightest weight equipment. No dacron or kapok stuffed sleeping bags for him—nothing but goose down will do. No nice big wall tents or pop tents for the hiker; he must be content with a lightweight nylon tarp, a sheet of polyethylene plastic, or even no shelter at all. Of canned foods there will be none; dehydrated food is the order of the day.

After watching Bud in action and listening to his discourses, I became seized with the notion that no camper worth his salt was any camper at all—dared even call himself a camper—until he had gone out on a fourteen day hike, living entirely out of the pack on his back. I resolved to do just that. But resolution by itself was not enough; it had to be backed up with proper equipment and, although Iris and I had plenty of camping equipment, none of it was suitable for backpacking. At that juncture, buying a full complement of gear all at once was out of the question as it is frightfully expensive. It seems that the prices asked are in inverse relationship to the weight. There was no other choice but to take a page from Bud's book and make it ourselves. Bud has designed and made all of his equipment, not to save money, as his materials often cost more than a ready-made finished article, but because none of the stuff available ever quite suits him, and because he simply enjoys making his own gear. And so in the winter of 1962 our evenings became filled with manufacture.

First, we needed a tent, or at least a suitable shelter. Our pop tent weighs thirteen pounds cased, unthinkable tonage for a backpacker. For the shelter I used a big sheet of vinyl plastic; actually, it was two large rectangular pieces that had been heat sealed together—one was green and one brown, but no matter for that. Why be conventional? Either color was suitable for the woods; we had both. I cut it in such a manner that the shelter when pitched was three feet wide at the back. The sides were triangular and came forward from the peak in two triangular wings. Two shear poles sufficed to pitch it as they do a miner's tent. It was five feet wide across the front when it was pitched with the peak four feet high. It weighed just three and a half pounds and turned out to be an abomination. We never used it after its first and only trip.

Next to be considered was a pair of packboards. The packboard is perhaps the most critical item in the backpacker's equipment, and although the Trapper Nelson or Alaskan style was readily available and quite inexpensive, I decided against them. The southern European rucksack, so popular in Bavaria, is execrable for anything other than a weekend outing. Everything in the pack falls to the bottom; it slumps, it bulges, and it drags the wearer's shoulders down and back. The Bergans or Norwegian style rucksack has an aluminum frame which is a great improvement, but still it is not ideal, and good ones are costly to boot. By far the best of all are the Kelty packs and Kelty style packs of which there are several. These have aluminum frame supports which follow the thoracic and lumbar curves of the spine, the profile of the packsack is narrow, and the weight is borne on the point of the hip rather than dragging down from the shoulder. Unfortunately, the Kelty packs were way beyond our purse at this time; a pair would have cost about $70.00. A molded fiberglass packboard caught my eye in one of the many catalogues that I'd acquired, and I decided to make a pair of them.

Thus on a biting cold night in January Iris found herself in our basement stripped to the hips. I rolled a tube of stockinet over her torso and began to apply a body cast with materials purloined from the orthopedics department of the hospital in which I work. First the solid strips of plaster-impregnated gauze were laid on vertically for support; then the rest of the gauze was rolled round and round her until it was sufficiently thick. At one point I shouted at her, "Quit breathing, you're cracking the plaster."

"Well, when will it be dry?"

"In about fifteen minutes."

She didn't quite make it, but the cast dried properly anyway. After a time she said, "Hey, it's getting hot in here. When are you going to get me out of this thing?" Plaster of Paris gives off heat as it dries so this was not surprising, but it suddenly occurred to me, "How *am* I going to get her out of it?" I had no cast cutting instruments at home. I found an old pair of tin snips and began to snip away feverishly at the still damp plaster. It was hardening rapidly now and getting more and more difficult to cut. There was a long, terrible moment when I had visions of carting her through the streets of Ann Arbor on a freezing winter night, undressed save for a suit of plaster from which her arms were protruding at right angles. She was not reassured at the prospect, either. Luckily I managed to chew my way through the sides of the cast with the tin snips, and the two halves fell with a full thunk to the floor. "You and your silly ideas of camping," she said and stomped off upstairs.

The next week the cast was on the other foot, so to speak, as an orthopedist friend rolled a body jacket onto my stockineted frame. There was no need for tin snips this time as the procedure took place in the cast application room of the orthopedics clinic, and there were plenty of electric cast cutting saws about.

The rear halves of the two plaster casts served as molds on which to form the fiberglass packboards. A layer of Saran wrap over the molds prevented the plastic from adhering to the casts. The fiberglass fabric plus the liquid plastic cost a grand total of $7.00. The resultant packboards could not possibly have been more tailored to order. Iris made pack sacks out of duck material obtained from two old army officer's val-packs. The straps for the boards came from a pair of Duluth packs that had seen many a canoe trip. These items have been mainstays of our equipment as they work superbly.

The last project was the most complicated and fell entirely on Iris' shoulders. Our sleeping bags were the usual rectangular dacron filled bags. While eminently suited to most camping needs, they weighed about five pounds each and were quite bulky when rolled. We needed goose down bags, these cost about $55.00 each; better ones cost much more. I had bought a surplus parachute for $12.00 and decided that we should use the nylon fabric for the bags. It was not a good choice of material, and we knew it at the time, but it was there and already paid for. Although it was sleazy in the technical sense, having rather few threads to the inch, it was incredibly high in tensile strength. Parachutes are constructed of many tapering gore triangles sewn together, the fabric pouching out between the stays of the chute. As the material had been cut on the bias and sewn in triangles it was a seamstress' nightmare to try to handle it along straight lines. My poor wife, accustomed to sewing dress patterns accurate to a fraction of an inch, almost lost her mind as the chute material stretched and gave. I kept trying to soothe her with reassurances that sleeping bags should be loose and floppy, but she had a hard time overcoming the discipline of dressmaking. Though she set her jaw and answered in monosyllables my queries as to how it was progressing, she kept grimly at it.

The bags were constructed of an inner shell and an outer shell, the latter being distinctly larger in all dimensions. Between them ran a zigzag baffling of marquisette. In this way a series of transversely oriented triangular segments were created so that there were no through seams to let in the cold and the damp. Because the outer shell was larger than the inner, a poking shoulder or elbow could not push the inner shell against the outer thus creating a cold spot. Iris made up twin bags which were in the form of sleeping robes or blankets which mated to one another by a series of small grippers. Detached from one another and folded lengthwise they were two separate bags. Grippered together they formed a double bag. By mid-April they were ready to be stuffed with goose down.

Prime goose down used to come from Poland, and in this country it costs about $15.00 per pound. We figured we needed two pounds for the top bag and one and a half for the bottom. That seemed to be quite an expenditure just for a bunch of feathers, so I began looking about for a cheaper source. With supremely good luck I found a local bedding company that still had a very small stock of Grade A down with which they had stuffed pillows. They had switched to foam rubber, were no longer using the down, and the owner very kindly let me have what I needed for the top bag at $6.00 per pound. The rest came from an old feather comforter of double bed size and proved to be very fine down, indeed. The end result of all this was that we had two goose down bags, one for summer use and one for winter use, which mated to form a double bag. In colder weather we could sleep under the thicker half; in warm weather we could reverse it. The total cost was $37.00 plus a set of badly frayed female nerves. The male, however, was jubilant. We were set! The total weight of both bags was four pounds, and they readily stuffed into stuff sacks not much larger than giant-sized loaves of bread.

The only items we purchased ready made were a pair of boy scout three-quarter-length vinyl plastic air mattresses weighing about a pound each.

With the problem of equipment solved, and solved with a deep sense of satisfaction, I began to ponder where we might go for our summer's vacation.

About this time, and what in retrospect seems almost an act of Providence, I noticed a book review of *Guide to the Wyoming Mountains and Wilderness Areas* by Orrin and Lorraine Bonney. I promptly bought it. Although the Bonneys have written it with the needs of mountain climbers uppermost in mind, there is a wealth of information in it for anyone interested in hiking and camping in Wyoming. Their book cannot be recommended too highly. Reading it, I was suddenly confronted by a surfeit of riches; the problem now was not simply where might we go but rather which of the many wonderful places should we choose as our first attempt at this kind of activity. One paragraph sprang from the page as if printed in bold face type:

"Bridger Lake ... is the meeting place of trails. Here is the finest of cutthroat trout fishing. A pair of trumpeter swans make their home here. Stream fishing is excellent. Moose are abundant. Here is the Thorofare Plateau and country, usually called 'The Thorofare.'

"This area outside the SE corner of Yellowstone NP is the greatest of all Wyoming big-game hunting grounds. It remains wild and inaccessible because of the distance into it, although served by good trails."[2]

I read no further. The Thorofare it would be.

The next several months were punctuated by an unending sense of excitement, anticipation, sleepless imaginings of "what will it be like," poring over maps, reading and re-reading the Guide, endless discussions over coffee cups, ordering dehydrated foods, minutely planning meals—activites that must be familiar to all who have ever undertaken this sort of adventure. Those who elect a grand tour of Europe for their summer holiday go through the same sort of thing. They who are phlegmatic enough or sophisticated enough not to be tremendously excited in advance of a great trip are deeply to be pitied for they are missing one of life's richest rewards.

In Ann Arbor this fateful spring, we met and took an instant liking to another couple, Doctors Bob and Nancy Grimm, who vibrated on the same harmonics as we did and who were spending the summer camping out west. It wasn't long before we decided to throw in our lots together and to make an old-time "mountain man's rendezvous" at Bridger Lake, which lies about forty-two miles from the nearest road head. Bob and Nancy had decided to go in by another route than the one we chose and, what is more, they were to start in at a different date than we. As they left Ann Arbor in June and were camping all summer, we were very much out of touch. We heard from them now and then from various spots in Colorado, but the agreement to meet at Bridger stood, recognizing of course that an automobile breakdown or other unforeseen circumstance could prevent it. Should we manage to pull this off, a real rendezvous it would be!

The months crept by. From a cooperative dietician I obtained two #10 tin cans and two two-pound coffee cans and made bails of coat hanger wire for them. The cans nestled perfectly and, with an aluminum skillet with detachable handle, were to be our cooking utensils. They sat on the floor shiny, unsullied, and virginal. As I looked at them I felt much the same as they appeared, insofar as this sort of camping was concerned. We also bought a flexible wire saw with which to cut shear poles for our shelter. Firewood was to be "squaw wood," that which can

---

2 Bonney, O. H. and L. G. Bonney, *Guide to the Wyoming Mountains and Wilderness Areas* (Denver: Sage Books, 1960).

be picked up at random. The full-length three-and-a-half-pound axe that I always carried on canoe trips and which I'd never be without was to be left behind. I felt positively naked.

The last two nights before departure were marked by counting out endless spoonfuls of powdered coffee, salt, sugar, and the like, all of which were put into mylar bags. Recipes were copied down on cardboard and buried inside pancake flour, oatmeal, etc. The mylar bags were put into labeled muslin bags that Iris had turned out on the sewing machine. The packs were loaded, the sleeping bags lashed into place, and we were ready at last.

When John Coulter joined forces with Joseph Dickson and Forest Handcock, turned his face to the west again, and started back up the Missouri Rover, he had been away from home for well over two years. With his two companions he spent the winter trapping in the general area around the lower Yellowstone River. In the spring of 1807 he set out for home again. This time he got as far as the confluence of the Missouri and the Platte Rivers where he met Manuel Lisa coming upstream with a large party of trappers. Once again he turned away from home and headed back up the Missouri for the third time. Lisa built a fort at the mouth of the Big Horn River at the point where it joins the Missouri in what is now south-central Montana. In the autumn of 1807 Lisa sent Coulter out alone to contact the Blackfeet Indians to establish trade with them. Coulter went up the Big Horn River, probably turned up the Shoshone River to where Cody, Wyoming is now located, and from there continued upstream following the north fork of the Shoshone. At some point he crossed over the Absaroka Range. This was not unfamiliar territory to him as he had spent the previous winter in the northern part of the Absarokas with Dickson and Handcock. His exact route will never be known, but it appears that he crossed what is now part of Yellowstone Park. He gained the west side of the Teton range and swung back to the east. He was gone about a month during which time he travelled several hundred miles alone and on foot, although at one point in his journey he joined forces with a band of Crow Indians and probably rode horseback with them. Wintertime and deep snows come early in that part of the world; altogether it was one of the most remarkable feats in the annals of western travel.

Whether Coulter actually traversed the region we wished to visit is inconsequential; he had certainly been nearby, perhaps had circumscribed it, and the entire region is imbued with his spirit. We called it "Coulter's Country."

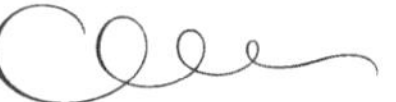

The route we chose to follow began at the south entrance of Yellowstone Park, followed the Snake River eastward to its source near the Continental Divide, crossed the Divide, dropped down along a small stream called Falcon Creek into the valley of the Yellowstone River, crossed the river, and proceeded one mile to Bridger Lake. There we hoped to find the Grimms who were coming in via a trail from Turpin Meadow, a spot on US Route 287, about thirty-five miles to the south and east of the south entrance of Yellowstone Park. Whether the Grimms had actually set out on schedule we did not know, a point which was to cause us much concern on the hike in.

Noon on August 6, 1962 found us at the park personnel quarters at the south entrance. The actual gate that admits visitors was another hundred yards up the road. We apprised the rangers of our destination and the route by which we intended to reach it. They noted our names and the date in an official log and kindly gave us permission to leave our car in a parking area next to their garage. We had a quick lunch, laced on our boots, shouldered our packs, and started off, ducking across the highway between whizzing automobiles that seemed to flash past endlessly.

Between us and the actual beginning of the trail lay an obstacle to be overcome—the Snake River, which at this point had already received the waters of the Lewis River flowing in from the north, and was one mean stream. The snows of the winter past had been deep, and the Snake was running high. There was a convenient ford a short distance downstream, but even there crossing by wading meant getting wet to the waist, a prospect we did not relish before we even set foot on the trail proper. Because of the number of people about in this populous part of the park we could scarcely strip to our underclothes as we did further in. Luckily, a large group of riders who, with charming modesty, called themselves "The Trail Riders of the Wilderness" were starting into the park about this time. We were planning to follow the same general route as they, except that they were going to take several wide swinging side trips that we were not. The main body of riders, about forty in number, had left earlier in the morning, but a few had stayed behind to finish last-minute arrangements. Several of them very obligingly permitted us to ride across the river on their horses. It was an enormous help to us, and we were most grateful.

Now we were properly launched. The trail ran off straight as a string through a wide, flat meadow to disappear in the lodgepole pines on the far side. We looked at it for a bit with a good deal of misgivings. Forty-two miles seemed quite a distance. Behind us cars nudged each other along the highway. In the Ranger station we had heard of a traffic jam up the road a mile. But ahead of us there was no one in sight. We hoisted our packs, yanked tight the waist bands that hold the packs snugly against the hips, and began our march.

We made marvelous progress for a full quarter of a mile before Iris demanded a halt. It seemed that her sleeping bag, which I'd lashed to the top of her pack in orthodox fashion, was pushing her head forward to the point where she had to look through her eyebrows to follow the trail. This would never do. When indignant, as she most assuredly was at this point, she can draw herself up to a full five feet, one inch in height. Neither her back nor her legs are very long, and there simply isn't much room on the former for very much of a pack. There was nothing for it but to lash the bag across the bottom of the pack where it protruded in an ungainly manner. Appearances, however, were not her first concern, and we trudged on.

By the end of the first mile or two my own pack had become something less than "a thing of beauty and a joy forever." It was unconscionably heavy and terribly uncomfortable in addition. At this point I didn't see how we could possibly lug those two monsters another forty miles although I was quite willing to die in the attempt. My fair spouse, however, had a much more tenacious desire to continue with life and much less masculine stubborn pride and, with the scant breath she had left, began to sound loud plaints to my rear.

"This is not my idea of a vacation! Let's turn back!"

"Take it easy, baby, this first afternoon is just a shake-down; it'll get better."

"Yeah, I'll bet it will. Let's stop for the day."

"But we've just got started. We'll never cover forty miles this way."

"Let's stop."

"OK. I'll scout for a campsite. There's no water here."

I charged off down the trail and in a short distance came upon a little stream. I reasoned that it would flow into the Snake River, only a short distance to our left. Such proved correct, and we made camp on the bank of the Snake only about three miles upstream from where we'd crossed it. What with the necessary adjustments to Iris' pack and frequent rests, it had taken us three hours to cover those three miles, a velocity that augured ill for the future of the trip.

The campsite was a lovely one; behind us was the edge of the lodgepole forest, before us the broad shingle of the river. The stream ran swiftly in front of the steep bank on its far side. Below us it disappeared in a sharp bend; above us was a short rapids. I pitched our shelter, got in firewood, and rigged my fly rod.

I had no sooner reached the edge of the river when I noticed an active rise taking place in midstream. I waded out and pitched a #12 Irresistible at the spreading rings. Instantly a good-sized fish arced up out of the water and took my fly on his way back down. I'd never before seen a rise quite like that and was puzzled by it. Despite his eagerness he missed the fly. I tried a second time and so did he. Again he missed. The third time we both succeeded, and after a respectable fight he came to the net. It was a mountain whitefish, the first I'd seen. I showed him to Iris and tossed him back. The rise continued, and in short order I caught and released six or eight whitefish. The stream seemed to be alive with them.

The mountain whitefish is really a large member of the minnow family and is equivalent in many ways to the chub in the east. Both are found in clear fresh water, often in association with trout. Both take flies readily. The whitefish, however, has much firmer flesh than the chub and, although somewhat bland in flavor, is infinitely more palatable. After a bit I walked over to the foot of the rapids and caught a fourteen-inch cutthroat trout on the first few casts. We could have had a handsome supper of fish, but we were anxious to eat into our food supply to lighten our packs as much as possible. All the fish were returned unharmed to the stream. I smiled to myself when I thought of a tourist we had seen fishing the Snake close to the south entrance. We watched him for about thirty minutes while we were waiting for the riders to get their horses to ferry us across. Though he plied his rod diligently, he never got a strike. Had he waded across and walked upstream a mile or so, he would have had all the fish he could have asked for.

The next morning dawned fair and bright; the river danced in the first slanting rays of light. After a leisurely breakfast and after more adjustments to Iris' pack we set off. I had given her one of the pads from my shoulder straps—it was quite unnecessary anyway as my pack rode so well on the points of my hips that the shoulder straps were almost slack—and we tied it to her pack to pad the lower edge where it contacted the back of her sacrum. She seemed to fare a bit better and we headed off.

The succeeding several days were variations on a common theme of fatigue marked by increasingly painful and blistered feet. I was wearing shoe paks with rubber bottoms and leather tops. In them my feet perspired profusely and my soles became macerated. Iris, wearing leather hiking boots, had less trouble. My packboard, of which I had been so proud because it rode on my hips, rode too well. The corners dug into the muscles above the points of the hips until they became unbearably bruised and sore. Both of us were generally whipped by the weight we were carrying; Iris' pack weighed thirty pounds, mine seventy. Although we had been cognizant of the need to cut out everything nonessential, our notions as to what was absolutely necessary and what was not were faulty. In the next few years we learned to get along nicely with packs weighing twenty-five and forty pounds respectively. I found that, for myself, forty-five pounds is a critical weight. Above it, the pack is too heavy; below it, it offers no problem whatever. However, we didn't know these things this time, and we suffered.

Our first source of difficulty was, of course, the excessive weight we were carrying, but beyond that was another, far more important. We were not only beaten physically, we were defeated psychologically. I had seen this sort of thing many times before in those portaging heavy canoes for the first time. One's ability to carry a canoe well depends almost as much on mental attitude as it does on physical ability. Though I recognized what was happening to us and tried to ward it off, it was insidiously undermining our morale. Poor Iris did not have the intense motivation that I had in wishing to see the country, to get to Bridger Lake, and to prove that she, too, was a *real* camper—all of which made the physical discomfort less unbearable. She could not have cared less and was on the verge of distraction.

The country we were traversing was the Yellowstone Plateau, a gently rolling, montane plateau lying generally at 7,800 feet above sea level. Patches of lodgepole pine freckle wide, sunny meadows. The billowing hills are covered with dense stands of timber. Though the scenery is not spectacular as it is in the Teton mountains just to the west, it is quiet, limitless, peaceful. Not a soul to be seen. The last shards of The Trail Riders of the Wilderness had passed us the first day, and then there was no one. It is ideal camping and hiking country, although some of its attributes were lost on us in our travail.

On our third morning out I missed a pipe which I had always treasured. It was an inexpensive member of the Comoy family but always smoked sweet and dry no matter how it was abused. Obviously, I couldn't bring along a dozen pipes, so I'd selected two that offered the best likelihood of a decent bowl. And now, the better of them, and the best in my collection was lost. Frantically I scrabbled about in the packs spewing food bags all over the landscape. I even yanked the sleeping bags from their stuff sacks hoping that it had got caught up in the folds of the fabric. All to no avail. I knelt in the wilderness and wept. At this point Iris left off what she was doing, walked past me to the nearby trail, and said, "For heaven's sakes quit your wailing. Here's your silly pipe," and with that she handed me a beautiful Dunhill that some luckless soul, a Trail Rider no doubt, had lost. I was flabbergasted but blew the dust and dung off the bit and popped it into my mouth. I have it still.

Toward the close of the afternoon the trail pitched over a steep bank and across the Snake, now a small, fairly shallow mountain stream. We sloshed across and decided to make camp in a dense stand of spruce, a most unprepossessing spot, for a prescient stillness had fallen that presaged a storm. We pitched the shelter alongside the trail, and just as we were finishing supper the first fitful breeze began to set the spruce tops into motion. Thunder rolled and reverberated up and down the canyon, the sounds bounding and rebounding off the confining stone walls. It was primeval, fearsome; we felt very much alone. Toward midnight rain began to pelt the shelter. As the front was open all the way to the peak, it wasn't moments before water began to run in along the underside of the roof and drop off onto us at convenient intervals. I rose from my sodden couch and spread the sides out, lowering the peak.

Outside the tent was a tumult of wind and water. We got wetter and wetter until we pulled our ground sheet from underneath the sleeping bag and spread it on top. By that time we were soaked through. In all my years of camping I've never felt so helpless. We spent a miserable night. Subsequently we learned to tie the ground sheet across the opening and peak of the shelter as a flap and rode out two more storms warm and dry.

Morning was marked by a slightly perceptible lightening of the gloom that enshrouded the spruces. Rain drops dripped from every needle tip and pattered onto the sagging shelter. We eased out into the wet, and my wife by some God-given talent of hers managed to get a fire going. As we sat there scrunched on a damp log, the woodsmoke pluming low through the trees, we heard a measured thump-thump-thump which then stopped. A yearling moose wishing to go down the trail immediately alongside of which we were camped had stopped about fifty feet off and was staring at us. We sat motionless. Finally, he could stand it no longer and made a break for it, running directly past and no more than ten feet away from us, to plunge through the river and up the steep bank. We were as anxious to quit the spot as he so we soon struck camp. As we left, I turned and dubbed the place, "Camp Dismal."

The day stayed overcast and cool, our spirits rose, and we made steady progress. Along toward evening the trail petered out in a miry spot where each of the many horses that had gone before had spread out to pick its own way through the ooze. On the far side somehow we got twisted up and followed a track which eventually ended up in nothing at all as all game trails seem to do. Now where in hell were we? We consulted the map trying to figure out our position by the contours. No help. We knew that the river was somewhere on our left, so we were by no means really lost; we simply didn't know our exact position. About that time I spied a tall marker pole and fifty yards from it another, beyond that a third, and the realization dawned: they marked the south boundary of the park. We followed them a quarter of a mile or so and found what was still the Snake River although one could have chosen any of several streams flowing together for the title. We were at its headwaters. It had been our best day as we'd come about ten miles, but we were very tired, and daylight had run out.

We had been eating steadily into our food supply and had not yet had any fish for supper though we carried only enough food to supply us with half our evening meals, relying on fish for the other half. At this rate, we'd have no more main dish by the time the trip was half over. I wandered about in the dark trying to get some trout and, though I had several good strikes, I caught none. Stumbling back into camp I adroitly stepped directly onto the rim of a bowl of stewed fruit that Iris had set out to cool. The air, which was bitter cold, became briefly warm and blue in my immediate vicinity. Iris was disgusted and amused at the same time. After a less than hearty meal we turned in.

The sleeping bags, soaked through at the foot the night before, had been stuffed into their stuff bags still wet—there had been no opportunity to dry them in Camp Dismal. When we first tentatively poked our shanks into the lower part of the bag, we shuddered with dismay. To our amazement the heat of our bodies dried out the down in minutes; the porous sleazy parachute nylon seemed to let out the moisture. We were soon warm, dry, and sound asleep. The next thing I knew it was morning, and I was awakened by the hoofbeats of a trotting cow elk. During the night the moisture in the outer shell of the bags had frozen into ice; I wondered what John Coulter used for a sleeping bag.

This day's travel took us past the end of the trail on Big Game Ridge, a much more direct route to Bridger Lake that follows the south boundary of the park. We had stuck to the Snake river and had swung in a long bight to the north. We passed through Fox Park where we found the remains of a corral used by elk hunters. Pink-sided juncos, pine siskins, and Cassin's finches fussed about the old campsite. The trail dipped sharply, picked its way through a patch of low, swampy ground and then climbed directly up a steep ridge about three hundred feet high on the far side. We labored up it under our heavy packs, resting frequently by bending over and putting our hands on our knees. The valley and hillsides we inched our way through had been the site of an old burn. Tall dead snags rose on all sides, beneath them an understory of low second growth. Woodpeckers, Clark's nutcrackers, nuthatches, and ravens abounded. Pileated warblers flittered about in the shrubbery. I was delighted; Iris was winded. When we got to the top, the trail still continued to rise gently. The scenery became more broken, more interesting. The protruding outcroppings of Two Ocean Plateau (Elev. 9,800') appeared on our left. Iris abruptly shrugged out of her pack.

"This is it," she announced.

"This is what?" I asked, though I knew full well by her tone what she meant.

"This is where we camp for the night."

"But, baby, it's only three in the afternoon! We'll never get to Bridger Lake this way!"

"I don't care if we don't. I'm tired out, and I'm going no further."

I was fit to be tied, but there was no arguing with her. The climb up that ridge had done her in. I was worried for fear that the Grimms were already at Bridger waiting for us, wondering where we were. We were making far slower time than I had ever thought we would. We discussed for the dozenth time the possibilities of the Grimms—where they were, wondering if and when they had ever set out, and if they were concerned about us. None of this would budge Iris at this point, however, so I set about cutting shear poles, pitched the shelter, and tried to please her by making a rock fireplace. Actually it was a beautiful place to camp, a green grassy spot with an open growth of lodgepole pines giving partial shade, the steeply rising rocks of Two Ocean Plateau on our left, a gurgling rivulet on our right.

When camp was made, Iris said, "Take your ill humor and get out of camp. Go fishing or something. We could use some fish anyway."

"Wonderful. Just where do you suggest I fish?"

"Why not that little creek?"

"Creek? Hell, that's no creek. It's a trickle."

"I don't care what it is."

"Look, dear, I know perfectly well that trout will work themselves into the most unsuspected places," I said with dripping sarcasm, "but they do need water to breathe, and there's precious little of it in that creek of yours."

"I don't care. Just go do something."

In fact, there was nothing to do but to sit and enjoy the lovely surroundings, but I was in too execrable a mood for that. I mean, My God, why did we have to stop so early? With a "what the hell" feeling, I rigged Iris' fly rod, a six-foot-long, two-ounce midget, and feeling like all kinds of a damn fool went to fish the "creek." I stood with one foot on each bank and looked with disgust at the water running over the cobbles between my feet. It was pretty enough and gave us an ample supply of cracking cold, pure mountain water, but to fish it was ridiculous. Nonetheless, I idly lofted a fly to a tiny pool. Snap! What was that? I couldn't believe my eyes. Something had flashed at the fly, but the water was so swift and so shallow that it had missed it. I tried again, holding the rod high to attempt to slow down the fly in the current. Again, it came. Snap! And an eight-inch native cutthroat trout had the fly firmly in his jaw. I shrieked with glee. Then began one of the most delightful afternoon's fishing I've ever experienced. It was so totally unexpected. Each fish caught was a triumph. In the course of two hours I caught eight or ten. Many more tried desperately to grab the fly, but there simply wasn't time or room enough for them in that shallow, racing brooklet. Some even tumbled over the rocks chasing the fly. I worked my way gradually downstream a few hundred yards and then worked back up. They were just as eager on the return trip. Finally I was abreast of camp. Here a small log had fallen across the stream, damming it, and creating a pool about four feet wide and eighteen inches deep. On this watercourse it was equivalent to a salmon pool on the Restigouche.

"By the Jesus," I breathed to myself, "it smells of fish." I knelt down on my knees about twenty feet below the log. The surface of the pool was smooth, and I knew any trout therein would see me. Working a short line out with a sidearm cast, keeping it over the bank away from the pool, I dried the fly and then flipped it to the head of the pool. It floated a foot or two, and then a trout rose and struck it viciously. He was a lovely, plump twelve-inch fish, the last for the day and the best of the lot. I was transported with joy.

Skipping into camp like a school kid I grinned at my wife. "What's for supper?" I asked.

"I don't know yet, what do you want?"

"These," and I dropped the fish in her lap.

In the days to come we caught splendid trout, welter weight trout, but these gave me the most pleasure of all. When one expects to catch trout, he is disappointed if he doesn't. When the fish are unexpected, they are all the better therefore.

The next day saw us over the Continental Divide, at this point a gentle height of ground at 8,600 feet elevation. Monkshood bloomed in purple profusion alongside the trail. Engelmann spruce adorned the slopes. On the way to the divide we passed several small beaver ponds on the creek alongside which we had camped. I longed to stop and fish them, but time forbade. As we crossed the divide we spied some high ground off in the distance but didn't remark it at the time. Falcon Creek soon appeared on our left, and for the first time we were walking downstream rather than upstream. More beaver ponds appeared—lonely, unfished-looking beaver ponds. To this day I wonder what surprises they might hold.

We stopped for lunch about eleven o'clock. The mosquitoes were bad, and my feet were worse. They had bled into the blisters and between the layers of skin under the blisters. The trail seemed to know no end. "Baby," I said to Iris, "if it weren't for the Grimms, I think I would quit right here and now."

"Well, why don't we? What's so important about getting to Bridger Lake?"

"If the Grimms are there and we don't show, they'll be frantic."

"But we don't even know if they ever set out. They could have had a car breakdown or something else. They might not be anywhere near here."

"I know, but we can't take that chance. We've got to go on."

"Never, never again will I ever set out on a trip where we've *got* to be somewhere at a certain time. It takes all the joy out of everything."

Actually, my real reason for persisting was simply that I'd been taught in canoe tripping that when one set out for a given point, by God, he got there come hell or high water. It was a pact that one made with himself. To renege was to sacrifice integrity. I'd tried once to explain this to Iris, but she, genuinely feminine, regarded it as senseless. We both persist in our notions, and it's a frequent source of abrasion on our camping trips.

"What if Lewis and Clark had given up ...?"

"You're *not* Meriwether Lewis! In fact, there's nothing merry about you." At this point, I certainly had to agree.

We groaned into our packs and hoisted ourselves to our feet. The first few steps were dreadful, after that they were merely painful. The trail slanted on and on and on down through a great growth of lodgepole pines. Several miles farther on it began to descend steeply.

"Thank God we're not climbing up this mountain," I remarked. The trail plunged down the hillside; half-running we suddenly burst out of the lodgepole into the open sunlight and stopped dead in amazement.

On expansive lines the country opened up, a mile, two miles, a broad, flat, verdant valley stretched away before us to be lost in misty horizon, on either side the walls soared up and up to nine thousand, ninety-five hundred, ten thousand feet, over all a bright blue sky dotted with fleecy cumulus clouds. We were overcome. We were in the valley of the Yellowstone River; in the distance, barely visible, Bridger Lake glinted in the sun. Forgotten were the sore feet, we leaped, shouted, hugged each other, and set out with new purpose in our strides. The flat country melted beneath our feet, we forded the river, hiked up the trail for Bridger Lake, walked up the shore till we found the Grimm tent, threw off our packs, and set up our shelter alongside theirs. It had taken us six and a half days, six really, as it was still very early afternoon, and we had covered forty-two miles. We had averaged seven miles a day which wasn't too bad, all things considered.

Since our return we've invariably been asked, "How long did it take you?" We don't think that's important. We know now that we can hike fifteen miles a day, but it isn't much fun. One wants to have time to fish creeks he can straddle, to linger over campfires, to photograph wild flowers, to look at and listen to birds. One wants to have time to collect memories.

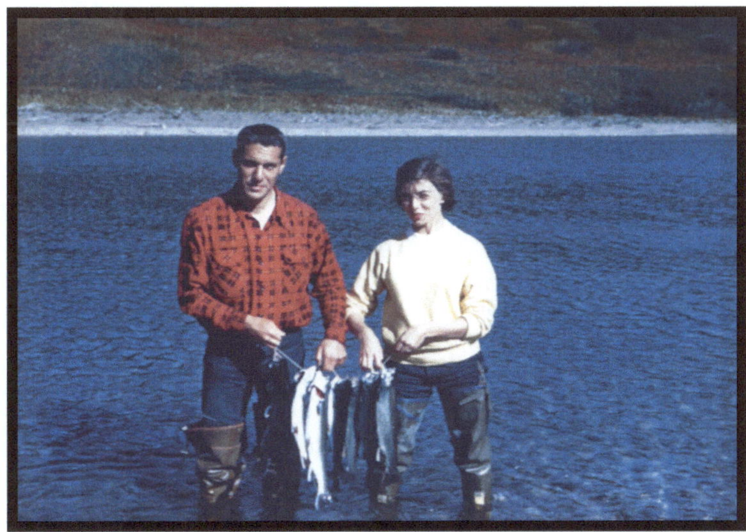

Jerry and Iris

SUSAN ELIZABETH ELLIOTT

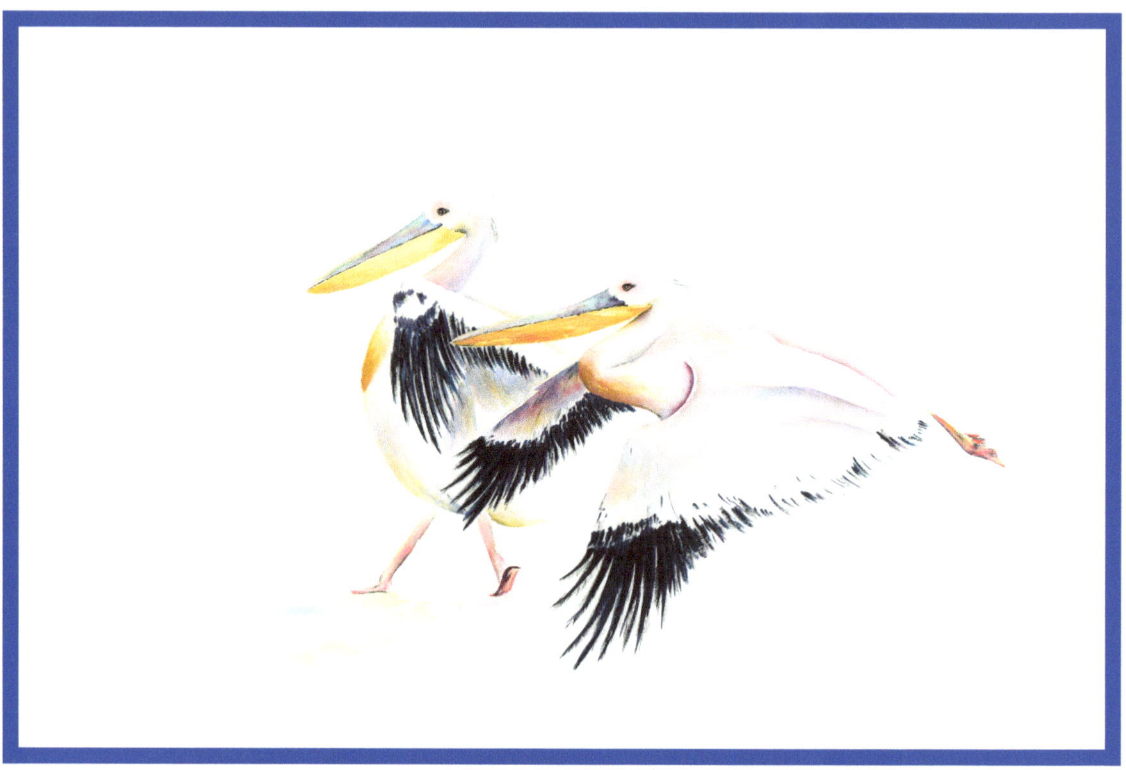

Pelicans, 2010, 14" x 22", watercolor, Private Collection

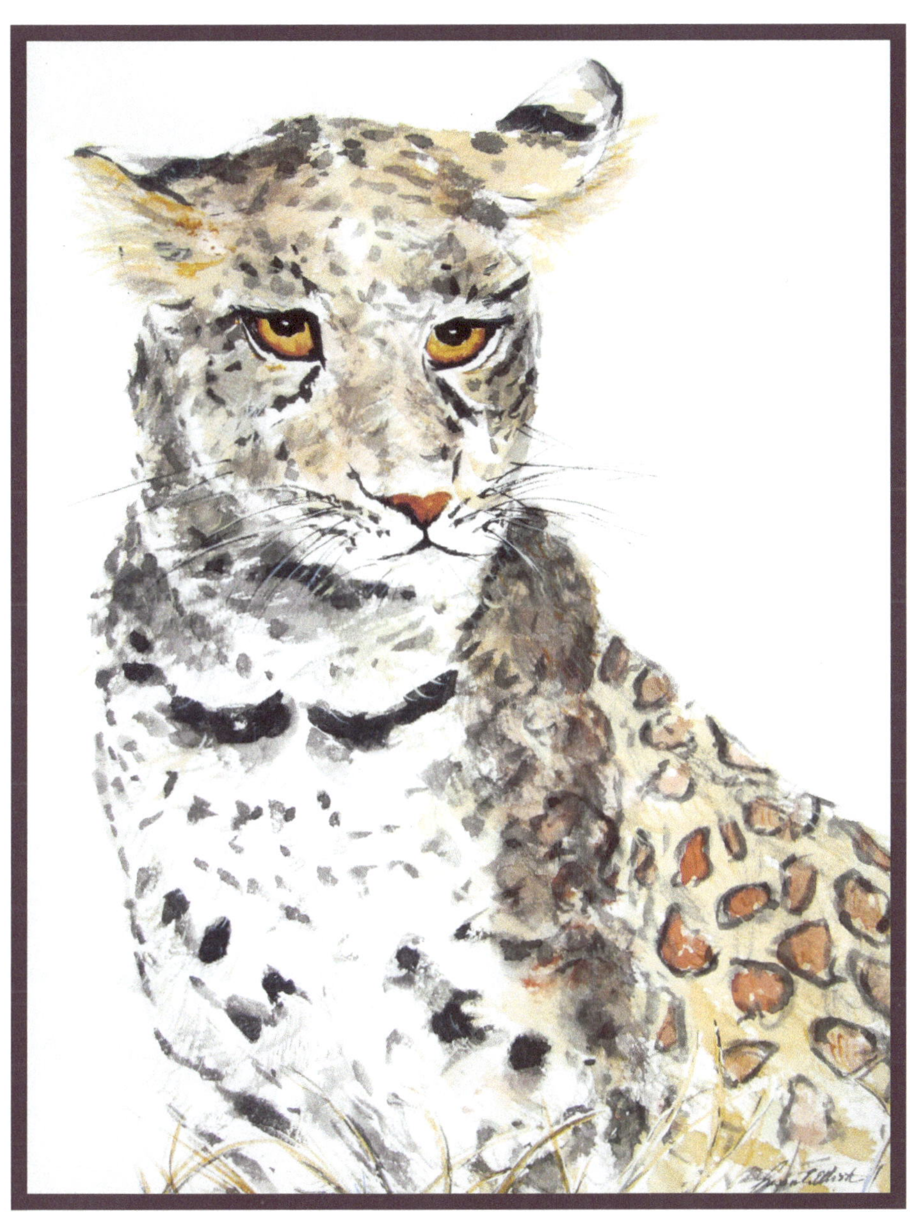

Leopard, 2010, 11.5" x 15", watercolor, Private Collection

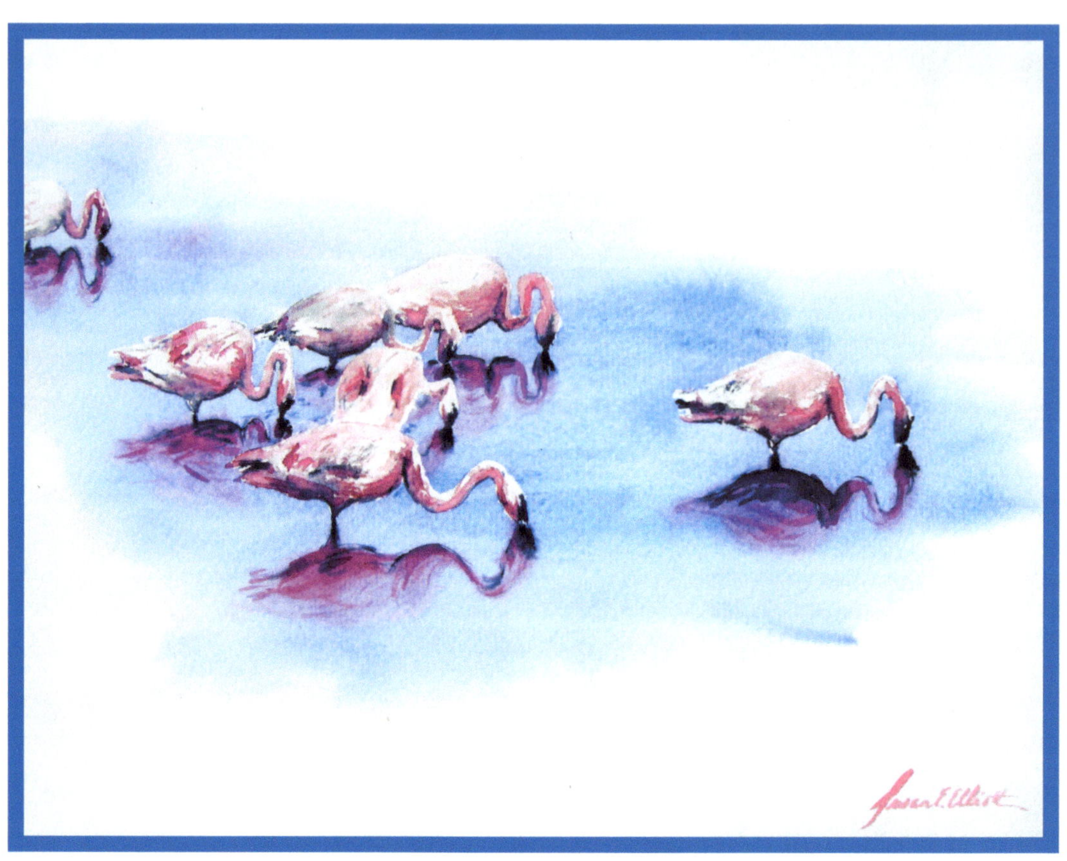

Flamingos, 2010, 11" x 14", watercolor

KEN FONTENOT

His Eyes

Last night I appeared in my father's dream.
He told me so this morning, having wakened
all sweaty. I ask for details.
He says it was a bad dream,
and he'd rather not elaborate.
He says I'd better understand the world
somewhat from a woman's point of view
because the anima elicits mystery.
Lovely mystery.
His life has been like clouds passing,
one after another, sometimes white,
sometimes dark and stormy.

Last night I appeared in my father's dream.
This morning he cooked fried eggs for me.
Made toast. Buttered it. Poured me coffee.
Gray-haired, he stands calmly near the stove—
whistling, talking about love.
The light has started to take over the kitchen.
Such metaphysics. Cannot be agreed on.
So I have to admire him, a messenger
bearing at times good news, at times bad.

Last night I appeared in my father's dream.
Jesus how bright his eyes are.

I Plan to Go to Germany

A sky so blue the birds stand out.
What stands out too, a sun, a moon.
One and only one of each of them.
A gift is what I'd call this air.
So given it reminds us thus
of things beyond our need to sell.
If air belongs to everyone,
what price is there to talk about?
Any landscape reminds the self
of truth—what is or what is not.
I'm here, a town I'd never thought
to call my own. The strangeness of
the light, the profound strangeness of
the shadows means another night
has come and gone, my life a life
that wants only to age as well
as cheese. Today I'm fifty-seven.
I think of resolutions still
to make, of fathers whose sons have run
away from home. My country's sad,
I plan to go to Germany.
I know men, and I know their ways.
Marriages fall apart and still
they rise to cook their scrambled eggs.
Another wish, another journey.
So our lives remain largely our own.

FRANCINE MARIE TOLF

Someone is Beating a Woman

yet my coffee tastes delicious and my dreams were sweet as the slap of a man in charge who throws me against the wall and takes me but does not split my lip or break my nose, that is not sexy. It's sexy that lures, that country between tender and brutal: *don't go there*, we say when someone steps near our tinder, *don't go there*. It's not them we're warning. I've longed for years to stamp on the landmines I've buried, let the remains of my decency flutter like ash to the ground, but someone is beating a woman, punching her face, spit glitters, blood undelectable muddies the hands I imagine cupping my buttocks, my breasts, hands I created that want me that force

Poetry Remembers

"Poetry ought to have a mother as well as a father."—Virginia Woolf

I had a mother. The smell of earth after rain
mattered more to her than glory on battlefields.
Loneliness loved her. So did sorrow:
she befriended them both. *Men will tell you*
I never existed, she whispered to me once,
but the little that you remember about me
will be enough. Enough for what, I asked,
wanting only to stay in her arms
and bury my face in her hair,
which was fragrant and wild
as language, before language
became words.

CY DILLON

Book Review: Nine Acres, *by Nathaniel Perry*

Nathaniel Perry. *Nine Acres*. Philadelphia: American Poetry Review, 2011. 60 pages. ISBN: 9780983300816. $23.00 (hardcover).

Discussing repetition in rhyme and meter Ezra Pound at his pontifical best said, "There is no particular voodoo or sacrosanctity about symmetry. It is one of many devices, expedient sometimes, advantageous sometimes for certain effects."[1] It is quite clear that Nathaniel Perry has achieved just the right effect with his use of a form composed of four quatrains of rhymed tetrameter for each of the fifty-two poems in *Nine Acres*. The consistency of form, which complements the consistency of the poet's focus on land, family, cultivation, and the environment, never becomes cloying or forced because Perry keeps the meter true to the complexity of American speech. This accomplishment, which is even more evident at one of Perry's readings, is not a small thing, no matter how easily Pound would seem to dismiss it. Consider this first stanza from "Tools."

My hands for pulling grass around
the carrots. A blade for poplar seedlings
that shouldn't have seeded there. My foot
for pokeweed and the pleasure of weeding

The first line may be regular iambic tetrameter, but after that, nature breaks loose and sing-song has no chance. Also reflected in this passage is Perry's avoidance of ending sentences on the fourth line of the first three stanzas in most of the poems, pulling the reader along and slightly diminishing the emphasis on the end rhyme. Again, this makes

1 Pound, E., *ABC of Reading*. (New York: New Directions, 1960).

for syntax that is consistent with the language we speak and that rests easily within the framework of the form.

In spite of the mastery of a strict form, the book does not seem to have been written as an exercise in the New Formalism. It is rather a very good example of a poet's understanding the value of structure and form and using that knowledge to his advantage. Perry wants to write about his experience working land and participating in family life in a rural setting without sentimentalism or the usual clichés, and the form he chooses helps keep him within those self-imposed boundaries. After all, to drag another twentieth-century poet into this, it is not just the net that makes tennis. The court delineates a space where the skill, intelligence, and conditioning of the players create a separate world. The players' implied agreement to follow the rules is also essential, and it is Perry's focus in following the rules he creates for his book, both in the form and the subject matter, that I find so compelling.

Here is a poet who finds a world of ideas in things, who finds enough characters in a wife and child and one neighbor to populate the book's world, and whose modesty of language and acceptance of the limits of his knowledge create a consistent, mature tone. As the poem "Introduction" suggests, Perry expects no unearned revelation from the land and life he has chosen. Writing of a coyote that "opened and shut / and opened again the woods' dark doors," he says:

... I tried just to read the animal's
face. But all I got was starkness
of form: that which hunts before me,
that which is not dark in the darkness.

In the same vein he accepts the inevitable failures of growing crops and enjoys the successes without burdening them with moral implications or the suggestion of metaphysical significance. The soil and trees are material soil and trees, and the human relationships that are addressed in the book are strong and important without the varnish of romanticism or nostalgia. Thus the discipline of form is matched with the book's discipline of voice and vision.

Some readers have compared the regularity of the verse in *Nine Acres* to rows in a garden, and the repetition of rows of weeks in a calendar is suggested by the number of poems included. We know from Marie Howe's introduction, written to recognize *Nine Acres* as the 2011 winner of *The American Poetry Review*'s Honickman First Book Prize, and from Perry's acknowledgments, that this book was inspired by M. G. Kains' *Five Acres and Independence*. But *Nine Acres* is also in a tradition that goes back at least to Hesiod's *Works and Days* and Virgil's *Georgics*. It is a serious book about practical living that addresses the human condition, but Perry, as surely as he avoids the sentimentality we identify with the pastoral tradition also avoids didacticism and moralizing. Of course, I do an injustice to the book to suggest that it is good because of what Perry avoids. Its value is in his ability create poems that approach Thoreau's "true account of the actual," and that certainly is "the rarest poetry." The book ends as well as it began:

> *... What did Kains, his skiff*
>
> *of a book shored up, his harvest stored*
> *for winter, need me to know of knowledge?*
> *That in seed and land we find an anchor,*
> *and in language we weigh out our courage.*

DON THOMPSON

Buena Vista Slough (1)

In less than one square mile from here,
so many birds are singing, unheard,
that if each note weighed an ounce,
their songs would add up to tons.

Not to mention incessant insect chatter—
hiss and buzz and crackle like fire.
If we could hear that, we'd think
the whole world is burning.

And maybe it is ...
That invisible conflagration could be
the light we see by
when we close our eyes in the dark.

And maybe it's all the birds singing,
that inaudible ballast,
not gravity, that holds us down
so we don't drift away from ourselves.

Crow

Crows never make excuses,
unlike us—but like us
complain bitterly about their blessings.

This one beside the road,
dissatisfied with the leftover rabbit
I killed for him yesterday,

squawks at the cosmos without thinking,
anymore than we do,
how easy life is for him—

compared to rabbits, so undemanding,
for whom every run is a risk
neither man nor crow would take.

DIANE M. MOORE

Carson City, Nevada

I could live here
under the rock outcroppings
away from the hot summer wind;
the sun would make me a cover
and I would become dry and brief,
my words sharp as the sage
skirting the Sierra foothills;
I could live like a mountain lizard,
scuttle with the ground squirrels
at the sound of footfalls,
suffering no invasion on the desert's face;
I could live here
where my heart could dry out
from a lifetime of heavy mistrust;
I would believe the night stars,
sleep in a grove of cottonwoods
rustling dryly,
feeling only kinship.

Breakthrough

Dreaming of a child drowning,
sinking into dark sludge,
my hand reaching for him,
I awaken to loud laughter,
the ridicule of pileated woodpeckers.
Through the window I see red tufts dancing,
envious crows watching
gay birds that rival their size,
boring excavations into dead trees,
feasting on ants, captured beetles
wrens will share later.

Seeing the magnificent birds released me
from the psyche's vain prophecies,
questions: Why am I here?
What is my intention?
the red tufts dancing,
their laughter slicing through
the Cumberland's gray smoke,
a small moment without aspiration,
everything coming to me
in a single look at them.

LARRY FOGG

Fractals: The Geometry of Nature

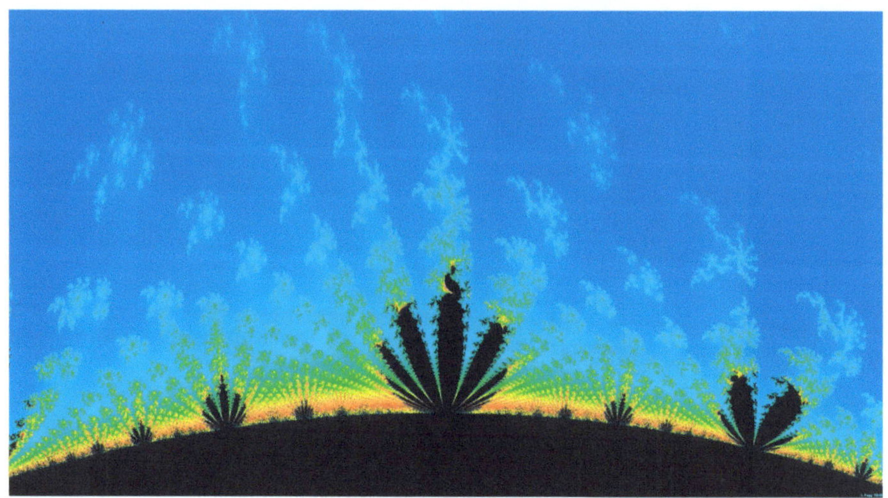

The Nature of Fractals

Imagine an engineer, working freehand on a sketch pad, designing a high rise. Or an artist capturing the beauty of nature using a ruler and compass. We know that both scenarios are inappropriate. An engineer needs precise and accurate lines, angles, and curves for his work. And nature doesn't use straight lines and perfect circles.

Thus, each (engineer, nature) requires a different set of tools. Euclidean geometry, the system of the engineer, is very useful for describing the things people make, but it doesn't work well for the things nature makes.

Which leads us to fractals.

Fractal geometry has been called "the geometry of nature" because it does a good job of drawing objects like galaxies, mountains, trees, and blood vessels. Fractals are infinitely detailed and self-similar. That means that as you zoom in on the image, the smaller details resemble the large scale shapes.

Mathematician Benoit Mandelbrot[1] coined the term "fractal" in 1975 to describe this new geometry.

Mandelbrot considered the length of the English coastline. From space, we can approximate a length for it, but we'll miss details that can't be seen from that distance. Using aerial photography, smaller bays and points come into view, and the measured coast length grows. A walk along the shore gives an even greater length. As we zoom in, our ruler gets shorter, we see more details, and the length grows. Try the same thing with a straight line segment 10 yards long. Regardless of the length of our ruler, the length is always 10 yards, since the line is a perfectly straight one-dimensional object. No matter how closely we look, no new details appear.

So the measured coastal length increases as the length of our ruler decreases!

The rougher the coastline, the more rapidly the measured length increases. We can determine a "fractal dimension" based on the rate of this increase in length. This fractal dimension measures the roughness of an object. Our straight line segment always has the same length. Its fractal dimension is 1, the same as its topological dimension. The English coastline has a fractal dimension of 1.2 or so. I once measured the fractal dimension of the Deschutes River as it winds through central Oregon. At 1.25 it was slightly greater than the English coast. So, fractally speaking, the Deschutes is rougher than the English coast.

Coastlines, mountains, and trees can be modeled with geometric fractals. This kind of fractal grows by applying a rule at ever smaller scales. The rule might be how branching occurs. A 90-degree branch makes a good ponderosa pine, and at 30 degrees the fractal tree looks more like the western hemlocks up in the Cascades. Another example of a geometric fractal removes the center portion of a rectangle, then removes the centers of the remaining, smaller rectangles, and on and on. This is a Sierpiński carpet,[2] and if you tear apart your cell phone you'll probably find one inside. Sierpinski carpets make excellent antennae.

1 Benoit Mandelbrot, 1924-2010, a French-American mathematician born in Poland.

2 The Sierpiński carpet is a plane fractal first described by Wacław Sierpiński in 1916. The carpet is a generalization of the Cantor set to two dimensions.

How to Roll a Fractal

The rule for creating the Mandelbrot set (a specific fractal named for Benoit Mandelbrot) is mathematical instead of geometrical. (See the *Pinyon Review* title page for an example Mandelbrot set fractal.)

We draw the Mandelbrot set using a process similar to a feedback loop in a sound system. Jimi plays a note on his guitar, which is amplified, picked up by his guitar strings, re-amplified, picked up by the strings again, re-amplified again, and on and on.

For the fractal image, each point, or pixel, has two numbers (or coordinates) associated with it: horizontal and vertical locations. We take the point's coordinates and plug them into a math function. The function spits out a new location and nudges the point to that spot. Then we put the new coordinates through the same function again, which gives the point another nudge. Thus, the feedback.

The function can be anything we want, but simpler functions lead to more interesting results. For the Mandelbrot set we just square the point's coordinates and add a bit extra (a constant). This idea of simple rules leading to complex results fascinates me, and it shows up in unexpected places.

The seventeen on (or syllable) rule for haiku leads to beautiful and deep poetry. The ancient game of Go has endlessly complex strategies flowing from simple rules. Yet, in contrast we can look at many large,

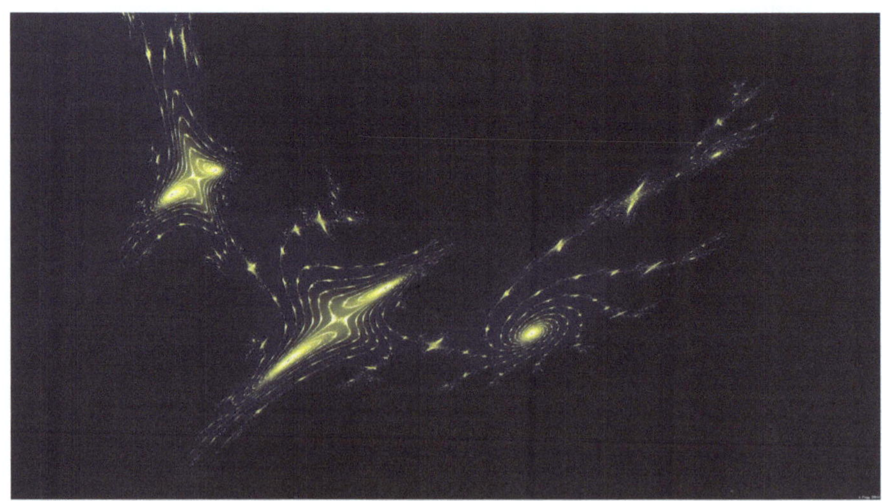

bloated organizations and see the stifling results of complex rules. Too many rules, like cooks, can spoil the company.

Let's get back to our point and how its wandering influences the feedback loop. Some points stay close to their starting location, no matter how many feedback loops they go through. These points make up the Mandelbrot set and are usually colored black (just because). Other points "blow up" after some number of loops. In other words they wander off to infinity. (Jimi's amp and guitar burst into flames.)

Points outside the Mandelbrot set are colored according to how many loops it takes them to blow up. We can do that coloring any way we want. Some points blow up after one loop—we might color them red. Other points blow up after 538 loops—they could be in the middle of the spectrum as a shade of green. And points close to the Mandelbrot set might take a long time to blow up—999 loops could be colored violet. Have a computer perform this feedback process to color each point in the image and you get a fractal. Zooming in on different regions of the fractal gives us an infinite playground for exploring the most complex objects in mathematics.

Each image involves a staggering number of calculations. When I started experimenting with fractals using high performance personal computers of the late 1980s, these images would have taken several days to compute; now they take several seconds.

Chaos Rules

For want of a nail the shoe was lost.
For want of a shoe the horse was lost.
For want of a horse the rider was lost.
For want of a rider the message was lost.
For want of a message the battle was lost.
For want of a battle the kingdom was lost.
And all for the want of a horseshoe nail.

Behind the beauty and familiarity of fractal images lies an idea which rules the universe in ways that you already understand. On a drive through town, you come to a yellow traffic light. You could make it through safely, but what's the rush? As you gently brake to a stop a truck blasts through the intersection. You have averted a threat to your life by simply choosing to stop at the light.

A commonly used example from the physical world is called the Butterfly Effect. A butterfly in South America flaps its wings and disturbs a bit of local air. That small disturbance spreads and grows until it finally affects weather in New York. If that seems far-fetched, consider two raindrops falling over the Continental Divide in Colorado. Inches apart when they hit the ground, one drains west to the Pacific and the other flows to the Atlantic. These "tipping points" are examples of chaotic systems, where a very small change in initial conditions can lead to wildly different results.

Fractal images include calm areas where there is little change and chaotic areas with infinite variability. Life has no equivalent of a fractal image that we can use to predict which moments are chaotic. You might think it would be nice to know that a particularly important moment is just around the corner. But we can't know, and that could be one of life's lessons.

The Math

The Mandelbrot set lives in the complex number plane, a fascinating place which includes imaginary numbers (Y and Q for this discussion) on the vertical axis, and real numbers (X and P) on the horizontal axis. The idea of imaginary numbers dates back hundreds of years but was slow to be embraced by mathematicians. In short, imaginary numbers begin with the square root of negative one. No such number exists so let's create one and call it *i*. If that's bothersome, remember that all of mathematics is a construct. People didn't like zero or negative numbers at first either, but they became extremely useful.

I said earlier that the Mandelbrot generator involves squaring a point's coordinates and adding a bit. More formally:

$Z_{cur} = Z_{last}^{2} + C$ (cur = current position; last = last position)

where:

$Z = X + iY$

$C = P + iQ$ in the complex plane

i = square root of -1

$Z_0 = 0$ (Z_0 = starting position)

And C is a constant whose coordinates (P, Q) represent the current point being tested.

We use this feedback loop to nudge the point around until its modulus, or distance from the origin, is greater than 2. The number of loops determines the color of the point. If the modulus doesn't blow up after some maximum number of loops (say, 1000), the point (P, Q) is in the Mandelbrot set and is colored black.

Expanding $Z_{last}^2 + C$:

$=(X_{last} + iY_{last})^2 + P + iQ$

$=X_{last}^2 + 2iX_{last}Y_{last} - Y_{last}^2 + P + iQ$ (subtract Y_{last}^2 since $i^2=-1$)

Separate the Real and Imaginary components:

$X_{cur} = X_{last}^2 - Y_{last}^2 + P$

$Y_{cur} = 2iX_{last}Y_{last} + iQ$

Here's a summary of how you could program a computer to create an image of the Mandelbrot set:

1. Get input from the user to determine the image boundaries in the complex plane.
2. For each point in the image:
   a. Calculate the coordinates of the point.
   b. Run the point through the math feedback loop until it blows up or hits a maximum number of loops.
   c. Store the number of loops for the point.
3. Use the number of loops for each point to color the image.

Finally, notice the squared term $[(X_{last} + iY_{last})^2]$ in the feedback loop. You might say this is a "non-linear" component of the loop. If, for example, the term in this position were linear (*i.e.*, a straight line), no Mandelbrot set or any other fractal can be generated.

Nature seems to require non-linearity for its most interesting behavior.

LUCI SHAW

Chiang Mai, Thailand

In his time off my doctor son
forgets bodies,
carves spoons. With surgical precision
he uses his little curved scalpel,
and though the wood is raw
and the shavings fall like leaves
on the floor around him
no blood is shed.

I'm watching the slow reveal:
sculpting, he uncovers
the spoon shape within
the blunt stick that he
used to defend himself today,
chasing away the wild dogs
on his morning run. Now he is renewed,
for tomorrow's long hours
at the clinic, treating the bleeding bodies
and panicked souls.

Wind

"the wind blows wherever it pleases ... so it is with everyone born of the spirit"

—John 3:8

How secretly the bones move
under the skin
and the veins thread their way
through their forests, the trees
of bones, the mosses of cells,
the muscle vines.

How privately the ears
tune themselves to music heard
only in the echoing cave of the head.
And the tongue in its grotto tests
the bitterness of unripe fruit, and wine,
the mouth feel of honey
in the comb. How cunningly our shadows
follow us as we walk.
And our breath, how it moves in
and out without great thought.
So it is with the spirit.

JACK STARR

Heroes and Villains

"I've been in this town
so long that back in the city
I've been taken for lost and gone
and unknown for a long, long time"
—Brian Wilson and Van Dyke Parks, "Heroes and Villains"

"The expulsion from Paradise is in its main significance eternal: Consequently the expulsion from Paradise is final, and life in this world irrevocable, but the eternal nature of the occurrence (or temporally expressed, the eternal recapitulation of the occurrence) makes it nevertheless possible that not only could we live continuously in Paradise, but that we are continuously there in actual fact, no matter whether we know it here or not."

—Franz Kafka, *Parables*

Two men sat on stools near a window by the swinging doors of the cantina. They had not seen each other in many years, and at first neither spoke.

Nathan Jackson stared out the window at something only he could see, across a tiled courtyard to a garden of carefully tended plants that met the sky where a pair of old pepper trees (*Schinus molle*) appeared to be in conversation. When the waitress, a woman who despite her light step was probably in her late forties, came to the table, he ignored her while William Reese ordered a pitcher of margaritas.

"Two glasses," he said, "No salt on mine."

He noticed she was wearing a sparkling silver cross.

"That's a beautiful necklace."

"Thank you. It was my mother's."

"What's your name?"

"Tina."

"Ah, like the establishment."

She nodded slightly. "Or the songs, *las canciones, cantiñas*."

Then she spun around and wound in the warmth went to get their drinks.

"Don't you know I love you," William said to himself, remembering how he and his friends once talked, following her with his eyes arousing feelings he once had. She reminded him of someone. Long ago. Someone put a quarter in the jukebox. Someone danced in the night unafraid. Head to toe.

So long ago. He rode the merry-go-round until he became lightheaded. He swung and swung and leaning back stretched his feet to the sky. Head to toe. Where were his childhood friends? Once in a classroom—must have been third grade—Miss West his teacher stood at the blackboard. She never married. At least he didn't think so.

"You remember how we used to say we were going to change the world?" Nathan said, still looking out across the courtyard.

"Ah yes, we were young, optimistic, and the girls were beautiful."

"But we hadn't seen enough of the world to know how hard changing anything would be."

"True enough, but even in the best of times, we can only help. We can't change people."

"But we thought we could."

"Ah, stand or fall, there shall be peace in the valley."

"But what can we tell them?"

"That perhaps we need two worlds to get it right."

The attractively built waitress reappeared with their drinks.

"Enjoy," she said, "My boss says these are on him. He recognizes you."

"Then I guess the next ones are on us," William said with a twinkle that became him.

"Something like that," she said and smiled.

"You married?"

"Well, my children were raised."

She paused, looking closely at William, then said:

"They started slow. I did as much as I could."

"Life is unpredictable."

"You can say that again. Twins."

"Two girls?"

"No, one of each."

"I hope they're healthy."

"Wealthy and wise?"

"If not, at least closer now."

As she walked back toward the kitchen, Nathan turned and said, "Do you remember that Mexican-Indian girl in El Paso?"

"Yes, I do," William drew the words out, as he imagined her in a short-sleeved blouse and skirt. Brightly colored. Innocent looking. Long legs. Her body fanned the flame.

"Yes I do," William repeated, "She was a dancer. Graceful."

"Well, she's not dancing now."

"When did you see her?"

"A while ago."

"El Paso?"

"New Mexico. Near the border, a diner. In the middle of nowhere with tarantulas for company. She remembered you."

"Yes. I suppose she would. We got along pretty well considering the circumstances."

"You should have listened to me."

"Ah, as if that would have solved anything?"

"Perhaps. She wanted you, you know."

"Marriage? Then what? I did what I could."

"Yeah, whatever. You never want to face the facts."

"But I did that time. They would never have let her marry me."

"There were alternatives."

"Why do you care? It was a long time ago."

The shadows lengthened with the dimming afternoon. Nathan stared out into the courtyard. William took a long sip of his margarita.

"They sure know how to make 'em here."

William glanced toward the bar, for another glimpse of the waitress, but she was still behind the curtained doorway. He closed his eyes. Her dress was low-cut, and he followed the slope of her breasts, Tina's, who had twins, not the other one.

"You remember *Rhapsody in Blue,* Nathan?"

"Which one?"

"San Francisco. That small orchestra near the mission. Where I was lost once."

"What about it?"

"It was hot. We sat outside. A jug of wine and thou beside me."

"What's your point?"

"I was just remembering how hopeful it was. The music."

"Hopeful? I guess that's one way to describe it. But Gershwin died young didn't he?"

"Yes, yes. Thirty-eight in '37 if I remember it right. He'd just composed those last tunes for *Shall We Dance*. Fred and Ginger.

The way you wear your hat
The way you sip your tea
The memory of all that
No, no, they can't take that away from me

The light changed. Someone put a quarter in the jukebox.

"Wind chimes," William said.

"What?"

"Hanging from the window. There."

"But there's no wind. You have to have wind for them to chime."

The waitress returned carrying a candle chest high and lit it at their table. Their faces glowed in the sudden light.

"Thanks," William said.

"Doing OK?"

"Sure."

"Well, let me know if you need anything."

"I need everything," William said, "and nothing. I get along without you."

Nathan said, "Never destroy what you can create. Reminds me of that argument you used to make. "

"Which one?"

"Your poem."

William closed his eyes and said:

Time had a beginning
A joyful noise

Come before the Lord
Who must have been

A time before
Time had a beginning

"So," Nathan said, "time has a beginning and a time before?"

"Something like that."

"A contradiction. You can't have it both ways."

"But that's the point philosophers have made for centuries. We do have it both ways, and we convince ourselves which way to believe."

William sipped his margarita. Someone put in another quarter. Someone danced in the night unafraid.

"You're under arrest!"

Both men laughed, the lines as familiar to them as they were to each other. Yet it was an oddness of William's and Nathan's lives that their friendship survived so long. Eventually, one night freed by a toke, William had insisted that the big bang theory was no better than a theory for God's creation of the universe. Nathan, who was teaching biology at the University of M--, had thrown his hands up and walked out of the conversation. They had gone their separate ways. Long ago. So long ago.

When had it started? Yes, that morning (muggy, overcast)—he had been in a particular hurry to get to his office. For weeks he had sweated the nuances of his presentation. Now he knew the pleasure the project had once given him would evaporate with the inevitable questions his more annoying colleagues would ask.

As he walked from the parking lot toward the two-story brick building, aging with moss and vines, he remembered the fragment of a dream from the night before. He was lying on his side. He opened his eyes, saw a pair of shoes nearby and put them on.

He stood in a well-lit auditorium, the one where he would make his speech. But the room was empty except for him. And dimly lit. The light came from a row of small windows below the ceiling. He fiddled with a device on a table. A projector? That would have fit the scenario, but it didn't look like one. Where was his computer? His presentation was there, clear, ready for mouse. And where was his audience? Had he arrived early? Or late?

"So," Nathan said turning to William, "suppose Kant was right that causality is not an objective feature of the world but instead something else, say a time-space grid, imposed by the mind viewing it?"

"Then I'd say the mind may create what it intends to discover."

"So you think it's all in our minds?"

"Not at all. I simply think that our minds affect how and what we see. We wear colored glasses."

A darkness was falling across the courtyard, and the enthusiasm of twilight's detail reminded William of Manet's painting, *Bar at the Folies-Bergère*. Why? He didn't know. One association led to another. Or maybe the inside of the cantina reminded him. It was twilight inside now. Some say it's the loneliest time. But no one stood behind the bar here.

Only the mirror, the bottles of white wine and pale ale, and two pools of light above them were similar to the painting. The stunning woman in Manet's painting, both facing us and in her reflection, existed long ago in Paris. And perhaps not even at the same time. The reflection isn't quite like the woman facing us. Perhaps Manet made them both up.

"Fell in love years ago with an innocent girl," William sang softly.

Nathan turned from the window.

"So how long do you think we'll be here?"

"I find it soothing, don't you? Try to keep the spirit high."

"No. It's oppressive. It seems calm now, but I have a bad feeling about it."

"Ah."

"Aren't you worried?"

"No, at least not at the moment."

William looked toward the bar, expecting the waitress to appear from the curtains about now.

"But I've been here longer than you."

Contributors

GERALD LEE BRODY (1931-1968) was an avid outdoor enthusiast; an expert fly fisherman; an amateur ornithologist whose keen knowledge of birds garnered him attention as an eight-year-old in his hometown of Youngstown, Ohio; a lover of dogs and horses and of his wife, Iris, and two daughters, Laurel and Alison.

CY DILLON is a college librarian who lives with his family on a small farm in Virginia. His reviews frequently appear in the *Virginia Reviews.*

SUSAN E. ELLIOTT is an artist and ecologist. Her watercolors recently appeared in *Open the Gates: Poems for Young Readers*, by Dabney Stuart.

GARY L. ENTSMNGER's recent books, *Ophelia's Ghost* and *Remembering the Parables,* intertwine fiction, philosophy, history, and poetry.

LARRY FOGG has an insatiable curiosity for nature, science, mathematics, and the out-of-doors. A free-spirited writer and computer programmer, he lives and plays in central Oregon.

KEN FONTENOT, poet and German scholar, is a native New Orleanian who currently lives and works in Austin, Texas. His most recent poetry collection is *In a Kingdom of Birds.*

DIANE M. MOORE is a retired Archdeacon of the Episcopal Diocese of W. Louisiana, living in Louisiana and Tennessee. A writer of fiction, non-fiction, and poetry, her most recent work is *Redeemed by Blood.*

LUCI SHAW, a widely anthologized poet, essayist, and teacher, lives in the Pacific Northwest. Her most recent volume of poetry is *Harvesting Fog.*

JACK STARR, with an imaginative talent for fiction and nonfiction, lives and writes in Southern California.

DABNEY STUART, a master of the English language and highly acclaimed poet, is the author of 17 volumes of poetry, most recently, *Greenbrier Forest.* He lives in Lexington, Virginia.

DON THOMPSON was born in the Southern San Joaquin Valley of California, where he has remained most of his life and where his most recent collection of poems, *Everything Barren will be Blessed,* is set.

FRANCINE MARIE TOLF's poems and essays express her deep passion for animals, nature, humanity, and language. A Minnesotan, her most recent book is entitled *Prodigal.*

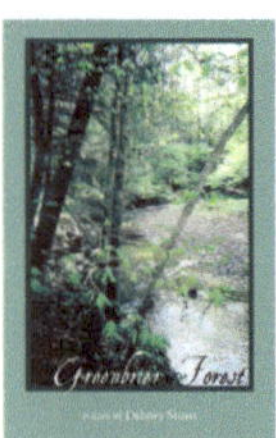

Greenbrier Forest 2012, 80 pages, $15.00, 978-1-936671-03-8

Poems by **Dabney Stuart**—Twice a year Dabney Stuart and his wife spend a week in a West Virginia state park. They often return to the same cabin in Greenbrier State Forest, where Stuart began these poems. The result is a series of meditations deriving primarily from the sights and sounds of Greenbrier Forest. Occasionally the work invokes other locations, as in "The flat arc of this ocean:" the speaker is watching the Pacific Ocean, but it turns out to be not all that far from Hart's Run in West Virginia.

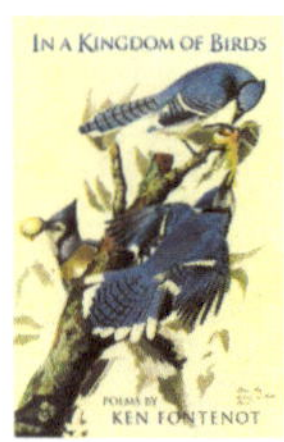

IN A KINGDOM OF BIRDS 2012, 88 pages, $15.00, 978-1-936671-07-6

Poems by **Ken Fontenot**—"Fontenot is one of the most original, moving poets in the world. I have treasured his work for years—his images startle us awake. His wisdom sears." —NAOMI SHIHAB NYE

"… poems self-aware enough to recognize that in all things exist both tragedy and light, but poems not so besotted with that conniving paradox to dwell too solemnly on it for too long. There's exquisite craft in knowing how to navigate those skies." —JILL ALEXANDER ESSBAUM

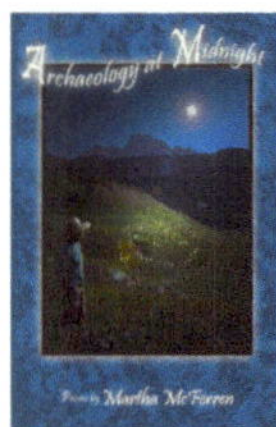

Archaeology at Midnight 2011, 96 pages, $15.00, 978-1-936671-05-2

Poems by **Martha McFerren**—McFerren looks for wisdom in the world around her, which includes the past and its narrative expression in myth. She profoundly feels that those before us were like us, that they mean something to us, even wrapped in the enigmas of distant times and cultures.

"I can think of no other poet who can inhabit the spirit, the world, and the lives of so many classical and historical figures and have them all conspire into a single, unique voice."—JOHN SKOYLES

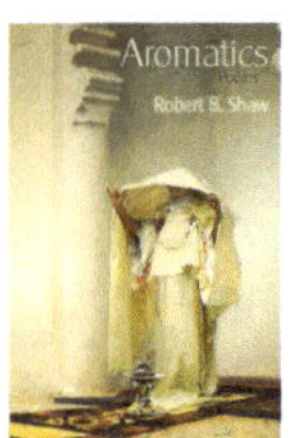

Aromatics 2011, 100 pages, $15.00, 978-0-9821561-9-3

Poems by **Robert B. Shaw**—The scents that permeate *Aromatics* include bittersweet ones of memory, acrid ones of danger, and others equally enticing or alarming. Shaw's scrutiny of the world's inner mysteries is revealed in daily concerns and the self-reflection and hope that accompanies it. Robert Frost offered this definition of a successful poem: "Read it a hundred times: it will forever keep its freshness as a metal keeps its fragrance." Shaw's poems aspire to that high standard.

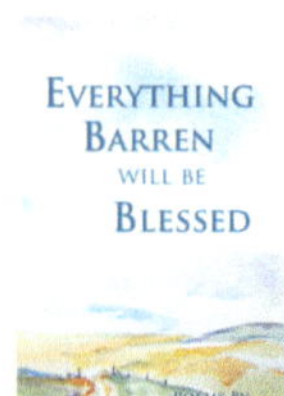

EVERYTHING BARREN WILL BE BLESSED 2012, 80 pages, $15.00, 978-1-936671-06-9

Poems by **Don Thompson**—Immediate and memorable images of hot Southern California valleys and desert inhabited by wild and civilized life—coyotes, hawks, pistachio and almond groves, humans—remind us of the importance of our relationship with nature and our mortality. Our isolation and our coexistence with nature are inevitable. Thompson's lifelong immersion in agricultural landscape is as clear as the water and stone in Preacher Valley.

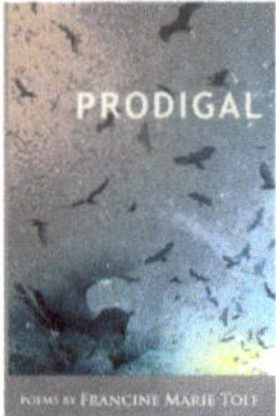

PRODIGAL 2012, 88 pages, $15.00, 978-1-936671-08-3

Poems by **Francine Marie Tolf**—Nature, animals, language, and discoveries that occur when one of these living strands intersects with another. Tolf doesn't shy from the savagery humans inflict on earth, but instead encourages us to reflect and understand if we can. Yet these finely tuned poems balance sorrow and outrage with deep joy and delight. Multilayered and intimate, *Prodigal* offers hope, derived not from cheaply won sentiment, but from an intensely personal conviction welling from an imperfect and compassionate heart.

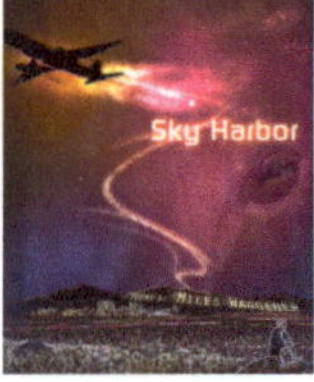

SKY HARBOR 2011, 84 pages, $15.00, 978-1-936671-01-4

Poems by **Miles Waggener**—"Read this book slowly; it is as breathtaking and suspenseful as our time here." —MELISSA KWASNY

"Collisions between desert landscape and air-conditioned condominium developments form a stimulating dynamic and an indelible backdrop on which the poet's major concerns—memory, the land's impression on the psyche, logos, spiritual longing—unfold, to distinct and brilliant consequence." —CHRIS DOMBROWSKI

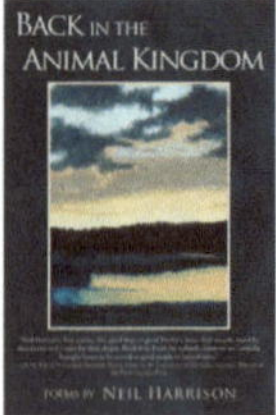

BACK IN THE ANIMAL KINGDOM 2011, 110 pages, $15.00, 978-1-936671-02-1

Poems by **Neil Harrison**—"Rooted in the immense landscape of the Plains, Harrison is attuned to nature and draws us into the terrain. He scans his memory for moments that remain clear and shining. He sheds light on his past and ours in celebration and sorrow." —MARIA MAZZIOTTI GILLAN

"… beautifully crafted, with just enough rhythm to deflect the craft. Individually and collectively these poems offer a marvelous and compelling journey into the animal kingdom …" —WILLIAM KLOEFKORN

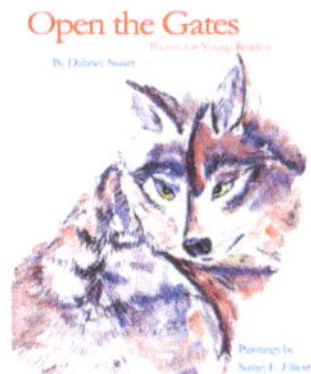

Open the Gates 2010, 94 pages, color, $27.00, 978-0-9821561-6-2
Poems for Young Readers by **Dabney Stuart**, Paintings by **Susan E. Elliott**—Rhinoceros to remora—the animals in Stuart's poems come alive in a spirit of playfulness. Adults too will appreciate the poems' intelligence, questions, and masterly use of the English language.
"Elliott understands the importance of space. The Chinese say space is where most of the qi resides in a painting. Elliott's pastel colors and delicate brush work invite a new outlook for children's art." —WINNIE CHRISTOPHER

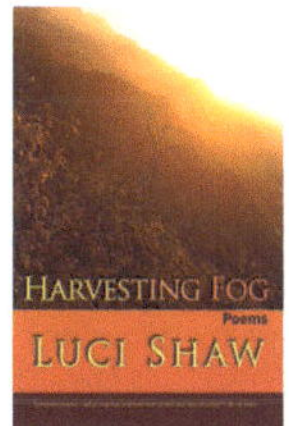

Harvesting Fog 2010, 104 pages, $15.00, 978-0-9821561-2-4
Poems by **Luci Shaw**—In arid coastal areas of South America, locals hang rags outside until they're saturated with fog. They wring out this water as a means of survival and call it "harvesting fog." That, writes Shaw, is a lot like writing poems. Shaw's poems satisfy a thirsty imagination and turn the details of our lives, the droplets, into music of possibility.
"Her poems draw deeply on the legacy she has embraced as an heir to Herbert, Hopkins, and Dickinson."—MARILYN MCENTYRE

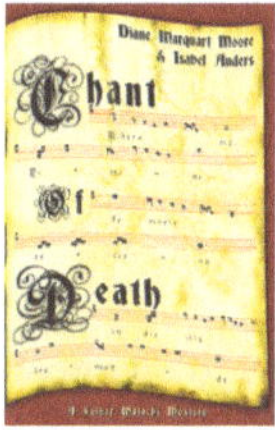

Chant of Death 2010, 152 pages, $15.00, 978-0-9821561-7-9
A Mystery by **Diane M. Moore & Isabel Anders**—The traditional Seven Deadly Sins are fleshed out in a complex, unfolding narrative of suspicion, darkness, and deceit. In a story straight from the headlines—of monks becoming "rock stars," *Chant of Death* is set in a fictional Benedictine Abbey in southern Louisiana. When murder breaks out, Father Malachi's powers are stretched to the limit in order to protect the innocent and identify the killer.
"A remarkable piece of storytelling."—DARRELL BOURQUE

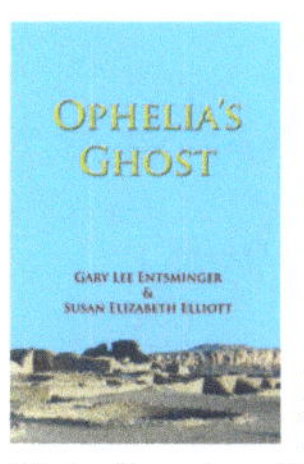

OPHELIA'S GHOST 2008, 292 pages, $15.00, 978-0-9821561-0-0
A Novel by **Gary L. Entsminger & Susan E. Elliott**—Eva Hail disappears from her campsite where she is researching the Anasazi abandonment of the 14th century. Joe Hill, a local tracker, is asked to look for her. Joe's daughter, Nina, is playing Ophelia in *Hamlet*, which introduces questions debated since 1958: *Can we know if we've seen a ghost? Can witnesses validate reality?*
"The book's best quality is the striking depth of the portrayal of the characters and their interaction."—CY DILLON

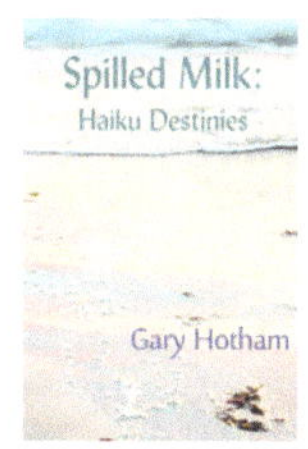

Spilled Milk 2010, 144 pages, bamboo art, $15.00, 978-0-9821561-5-5
Haiku Destinies by **Gary Hotham**—The work of a decade of noticing, observing, and writing, American haiku master, Hotham, asks us to see in the dark with our eyes wide open.
"Insightful, Hotham takes you into the true meaning of a haiku moment—that moment of awakening. Funny, quiet, meaningful, brilliant: these are the works of a haiku master." —GARRY GAY
"The images and words resonate beyond the surface into our own memories, associations, and consciousness of being alive." —RANDY BROOKS

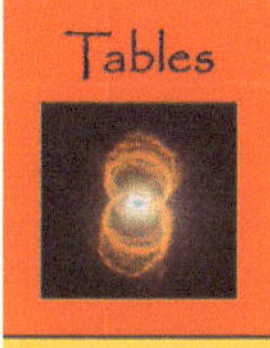

Tables 2009, 100 pages, $15.00, 978-0-9821561-1-7
Poems by **Dabney Stuart**—Nuclear physics to astronomy—Stuart uses images from these areas to explore dimensions of everyday human experience. In "Yucca Mountain," the place planned for the burial of nuclear waste becomes a focus for the yucca plant, the dances Native Americans performed on the little mountain, and the speaker's memories of his father.
"These poems move across the reaches of the mind … 49 poems cut and set so precisely that no mortar is necessary." —CY DILLON

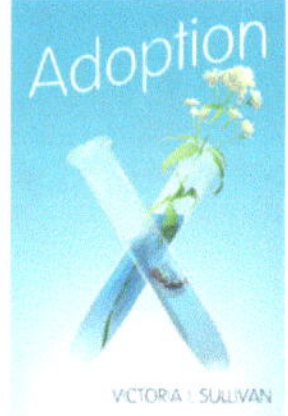

Adoption 2010, 172 pages, $15.00, 978-1-936671-00-7
Speculative Fiction by **Victoria I. Sullivan**—When six-year-old Mary's mother dies, she is "adopted" by her neighbors, Val and David. But nothing about Mary is normal. She's a giant—nearly seven feet tall, brilliant and beautiful, the result of her mother's *in vitro* fertilization. Murder, mystery, speculative science, and a mother's love blend in a novel that asks us to consider what would happen if life were just a little bit different.

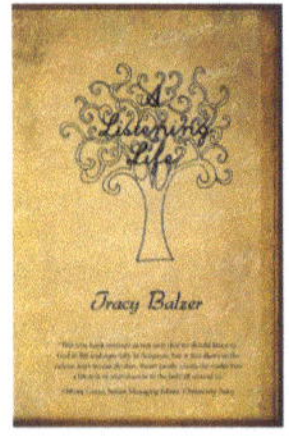

A Listening Life 2011, 112 pages, $16.00, 978-1-936671-04-5

Reflective Essays by **Tracy Balzer**—"Balzer not only discovers deeply enriching disciplines as she listens, she writes about them vividly, intimately, opening up to us her sensitive heart in a way that draws us towards the God she hears speaking."—Luci Shaw

"Wonder, attention, journey, stillness—*A Listening Life* explores the very lineaments of the spiritual life. Her book cultivates wonder and attentiveness—I found myself becoming calmer, more peaceful, and more prayerful as I read."—Lauren Winner

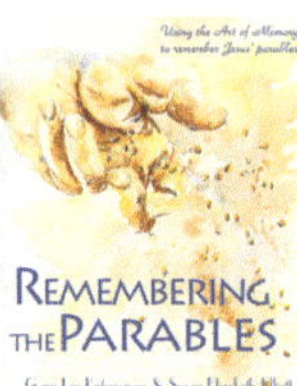

REMEMBERING THE PARABLES 2010, 160 pages, B&W illustrations, $18.00, 978-0-9821561-3-1

Using the Art of Memory to remember Jesus' parables by **Gary L. Entsminger & Susan E. Elliott**—The Art of Memory has been used for mental and spiritual training by ancient orators, Christian figures, and modern memory masters since before the time of Christ. It involves placing symbolic images along a memory journey. By learning Jesus' parables by heart, you will know them more deeply. By practicing the Art of Memory, you will grow to see your memories as treasures and enduring gifts.

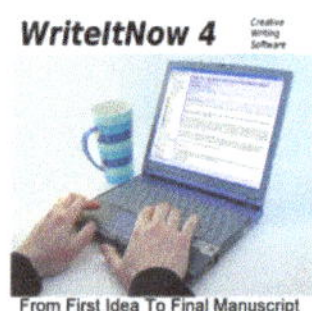

WriteItNow 4 2009, CD, $69.95, B002PRIT0O (Distributed in the U.S. by Pinyon Publishing)

Creative Writing Software by **Ravenshead Services**—

- Story board
- Writing targets
- Chapters, scenes, locations, notes
- Relationship diagrams
- Manuscript formatting
- Idea generators
- Readability, word count, thesaurus, spell check
- Submissions tracker
- Event timeline

You Who Make the Sky Bend 2011, 112 pages, color, $27.00, 978-0-9821561-8-6

Saints as Archetypes of the Human Condition, Lives by **Lisa Sandlin**, Retablos by **Catherine Ferguson**—Retablo paintings of saints, accompanied by biographies that draw on ancient sources, poetry, and literature—relating the saints to stages of the human condition, thus placing them into the wheel of life. For they touch lives. The saints remain on call. Many people talk to them daily. And many people believe they are heard—by the saint, their better selves, their own hearts.

EcoSim Professional 2011, Download, $49.95

Null Modeling Software by **Gary L. Entsminger**—*EcoSim Professional* is an interactive computer program for null model analysis of community ecology patterns (co-occurrence, guild structure, niche overlap, range overlap, size overlap, species overlap, species diversity, ANOVA, regression, chi-squared, and runs tests). *EcoSim Professional* randomizes observed data to create random null-hypothesis communities, then statistically compares the patterns in these randomized communities with those in the real data matrix.

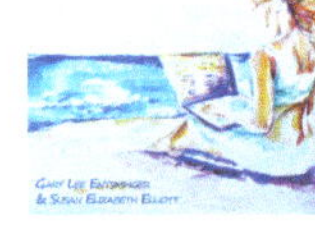

Making the Most of WriteItNow 4 2010, 112 pages, $16.00, 978-0-9821561-4-8

Software Guide by **Gary L. Entsminger & Susan E. Elliott**—*WriteItNow 4* is the ideal writing software for novice and experienced writers of fiction and nonfiction. From first idea to final manuscript, *WriteItNow* lets your creativity soar! *Making the Most of WriteItNow 4* is your key to effective, efficient software use. Learn to use the tools, get writing tips, and let your personal writing style flow.

PINYON PUBLISHING PURCHASING AND SHIPPING INFORMATION

ONLINE ORDERS: We accept Visa, MasterCard, and PayPal Transfers. All transactions are handled securely through PayPal. www.pinyon-publishing.com/books.html

ORDERING BY CHECK: Please make checks payable to *Pinyon Publishing* and mail your order to Pinyon Publishing, 23847 V66 Trail, Montrose, CO, 81403.

SHIPPING: We ship within 1-2 days via USPS Priority Mail with flat-rate shipping & handling charges:
U.S. = $4.95 (flat rate, 1+ copies)
Canada/Mexico = $12.95 (1-2 copies), $32.95 (3+ copies)
All other countries = $16.95 (1-2 copies), $47.95 (3+ copies)

PINYON WHOLESALE: We offer a discount for schools, libraries, & bookstores; 3 weeks for delivery. For more information, please contact gs@pinyon-publishing.com. Pinyon titles are also available through Ingram.

RETURNS: We do not accept returns unless items are not as described.

For more information, please contact Pinyon Publishing (gs@pinyon-publishing.com; 970-596-8676; 23847 V66 Trail, Montrose, CO 81403). Thanks!

www.ingramcontent.com/pod-product-compliance
Lightning Source LLC
LaVergne TN
LVHW070148110826
845147LV00002B/346
9781936671090